ted States, in order to form a more perfect Union, establish justice,
te the general Welfare, and secure the Blessings of Liberty to ourselves
uted States of America.

Congress of the United States, which shall consist of a Senate and House

bers chosen every second Year by the People of the several States, and the Electors
us Branch of the State Legislature.

the Age of twenty five Years, and been seven Years a Citizen of the United States,
all be chosen.

States which may be included within this Union, according to their respective
sons, including those bound to Service for a Term of Years, and excluding Indians
made within three Years after the first Meeting of the Congress of the United States,
d by Law direct. The Number of Representatives shall not exceed one for every
d until such enumeration shall be made; the State of New Hampshire shall be
Plantations one, Connecticut five, New York six, New Jersey four, Pennsylvania
th Carolina five, and Georgia three.

xecutive Authority thereof shall issue Writs of Election to fill such Vacancies.

ars; and shall have the sole Power of Impeachment.

tors from each State, chosen by the Legislature thereof, for six Years; and each

t Election, they shall be divided as equally as may be into three Classes. The Seats
d Year, of the second Class at the Expiration of the fourth Year, and of the third
cond Year; and if Vacancies happen by Resignation, or otherwise, during the
Appointments until the next Meeting of the Legislature, which shall then fill

f thirty Years, and been nine Years a Citizen of the United States, and who shall

but shall have no Vote, unless they be equally divided.
ore, in the Absence of the Vice President, or when he shall exercise the Office of

n sitting for that Purpose, they shall be on Oath or Affirmation. When the Presid
victed without the Concurrence of two thirds of the Members present.
removal from Office, and disqualification to hold and enjoy any Office of honor,
less be liable and subject to Indictment, Trial, Judgment and Punishment,

We, the People

THE STORY OF
THE UNITED STATES CAPITOL
ITS PAST AND ITS PROMISE

THE UNITED STATES CAPITOL
HISTORICAL SOCIETY

in cooperation with
THE NATIONAL GEOGRAPHIC SOCIETY

Washington, D. C.

1991

This edition of *We, the People* is dedicated to the memory of
Melvin M. Payne, founding member and vice president
of the United States Capitol Historical Society.

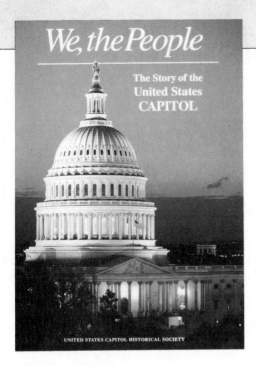

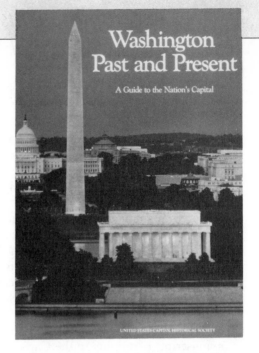

We, the People

Freedoms Foundation Award, 1964.

144 pages; 6³/₄" x 10"; more than 175 pictures, most in full color; foreword by Allan Nevins.

Lavishly illustrated, this guidebook traces the fascinating history of the United States Capitol over the past 200 years. Nearly six million copies of this book (now in its 14th edition) have been sold worldwide.

Washington: Past and Present

144 pages; 6³/₄" x 10"; in full color; foldout D. C. map; foreword by Warren Burger, Chief Justice of the United States (Ret.).

This beautiful volume deals with Washington, D. C., its history, and its present-day role as a seat of government. Illustrations portray the architectural, cultural, and recreational wonders of the Nation's Capital.

We, the People Calendar

26 pages; 11" x 11¹/₂"; 24 full-color photographs.

The Society's "We, the People" Calendar features outstanding color photographs of the memorials and historic sites of Washington, D. C., historical notations for each day of the year, and historical articles.

"A Place of Resounding Deeds"

A Narrated Videotape of the U. S. Capitol

32 minutes; in full color; introduction by Fred Schwengel, President, U. S. Capitol Historical Society.

Amid the grandeur of the U. S. Capitol, where Americans govern themselves through their representatives, narrator Cornelius Heine provides insights into historic events that occurred at sites featured in the film.

For information about our products, call (202) 543-8919.

Accomplishments and Programs
of the U.S. Capitol Historical Society

When the United States Capitol Historical Society was founded in 1962, President Fred Schwengel recognized the need for a handsome and readable history of the United States Capitol, America's proud symbol of democratic government. As a result, the Society made *We, the People* its first major project. From its initial printing, the book captured the popular imagination and quickly became a best seller. To date, nearly six million copies have been sold—a decisive confirmation of Fred Schwengel's clarity of vision.

Since the creation of *We, the People,* the Capitol Historical Society has continued to make highly significant contributions in a range of areas related to the history of the United States. Among the Society's most notable achievements are its sponsorship of original art for the decoration of the U.S. Capitol, its acquisition of historical artifacts and valuable manuscripts pertaining to the Capitol's history, and its funding of a fellowship program to encourage scholarly research on the building's art and architecture.

Reflecting a commitment to the study of history as a means of fostering and increasing "an informed patriotism," the Society's history department has published a number of important books about the United States Congress. At the same time, the Society has included within its programs a forum for professional scholarship and for the discussion of major themes in American history. It created a series of annual conferences devoted to an examination of the formative years of the Republic, 1763–1828. Topics as diverse as slavery, military history, diplomacy, the experience of women, constitutional philosophy, literary and cultural achievements, and the style of life in the 18th century have been explored.

The papers delivered at these meetings by many of today's foremost historians have been published by the University Press of Virginia in a series entitled Perspectives on the American Revolution. Numerous academic commentators have observed that these collections of essays constitute an invaluable scholarly legacy to future generations.

Ronald Hoffman

Symposia Director

Produced by the National Geographic Society as a public service

Robert L. Breeden, *Senior Vice President,*
Publications and Educational Media

Lonnelle Aikman, *Author*   Jules B. Billard, *Editorial Director*
Photographed by Joseph H. Bailey and George F. Mobley

Staff for the 14th Edition

Donald J. Crump, *Director*   Richard M. Crum, *Editor*
Viviane Y. Silverman, *Designer*   Vincent P. Ryan, *Production Manager*
Margery G. Dunn and Mary Ann Harrell, *Consulting Editors*

Robert E. Pullman, *Production Coordinator;* Jolene M. Blozis, *Indexer;* George V. White, *Director, Engraving, Printing, and Product Manufacture*
Cornelius W. Heine, *Project Coordinator for the United States Capitol Historical Society*

Additional photography: James P. Blair, Victor R. Boswell, Jr., Marie-Louise Brimberg, Donald J. Crump, John E. Fletcher, Otis Imboden, George Von Kantor, Joseph D. Lavenburg, Robert S. Oakes, James E. Russell, James L. Stanfield, Maria Stenzel, Rex A. Stucky, Mark Thiessen, Volkmar Wentzel *Lighting:* Nelson H. Brown, Larry D. Kinney, Philip R. Leonhardi, Joseph S. Stancampiano, and Kenji Yamaguchi

Architect of the Capitol staff members who assisted during the preparation of the book: George M. White, Barbara Wolanin, William C. Allen, and Pamela Violante

OFFICE OF THE ARCHITECT OF THE CAPITOL

STATUE OF FREEDOM.
The 19½-foot, 7½-ton bronze figure reigns atop the Capitol Dome (preceding pages). Sculptor Thomas Crawford planned Freedom's headdress to be the soft cap of freed Roman slaves. He substituted a helmet with eagle head and feathers to meet the objections of Jefferson Davis, who left the Senate in 1861 and then led the Confederacy.

Foreword

THE UNITED STATES Capitol Historical Society proudly presents this new edition as a service to history and to the American heritage. Revised and with many new photographs, the book tells the story of the majestic building that is our Capitol—how it came about, how it grew, and why it stands as a living symbol of the success of our Republic.

William Wirt Henry, descendant of Patrick Henry, patriotically reviewed that success in 1893 at ceremonies marking the 100th anniversary of the laying of the cornerstone for the Nation's Capitol.

"For more than a century," he said, "we have demonstrated, as no other people have ever done before, our capacity for self-government. Our federal system has been tested in peace and in war, and by violent forces from without and within, yet every fiber has stood the strain, and its perfect adaptation to our needs under all circumstances has been demonstrated."

Since then, evidence of the tough sinews that make a people great and strong has accumulated manyfold. And we can still agree with what a former Member of Congress, Rufus Choate, once said: "We have built no national temples but the Capitol. We consult no common oracle but the Constitution."

With such patriotic thoughts in mind, *We, the People* was conceived as a public service by the United States Capitol Historical Society. The book is published in accordance with the Society's aims as an educational organization—its membership open to everyone—to foster through the story of the Capitol an understanding of the richness and inspiration of American history.

Infinite pains have been taken to make the book an accurate and graphic portrait of a structure within whose walls a Government truly "of the people" has evolved.

The creation of *We, the People* in 1963 would have been impossible without the vision and encouragement of Melville Bell Grosvenor, then President and Editor of the National Geographic Society. This support has continued under Gilbert M. Grosvenor, the Society's current President.

The Capitol Historical Society is also indebted to two National Geographic Society executives, Senior Vice President Robert L. Breeden and Donald J. Crump, who have piloted *We, the People* through its many editions. We are thankful, as well, for the splendid work of the late Lonnelle Aikman, the book's author.

Above all, we wish to pay special tribute to Dr. Melvin M. Payne, former chairman emeritus of the National Geographic Society and former vice president and trustee of the U. S. Capitol Historical Society.

Dr. Payne secured the funds and talent to produce the first edition of *We, the People.* Its immediate popularity ensured the success of the Capitol Historical Society. Subsequent printings of the book through this, the fourteenth edition, were made possible by the leadership of Dr. Payne. His death in 1990 took from us a beloved friend and founder. Dr. Payne and his inspired stewardship will long be remembered.

This book, like the Capitol itself, is for people everywhere who cherish freedom. Here is evidence of the struggles that have been made to keep the ideals of equality of opportunity, of justice, and of freedom alive for all.

Fred Schwengel

President, U. S. Capitol Historical Society

MANUSCRIPT DIVISION, LIBRARY OF CONGRESS

GREAT SEAL *of the United States—an impression from the original die on a commission given George Washington, 1782.*

CONTENTS

INTRODUCTION

A Place

"IT IS NATURAL enough to suppose that the center and heart of America is the Capitol," wrote Hawthorne on a Washington visit in 1862, "and certainly, in its outward aspect, the world has not many statelier or more beautiful edifices. . . ."

The novelist saw the building almost complete, for the next year Crawford's Freedom was lifted atop the Dome. He could not then assert what all would say now, that the Capitol is the best-loved and most-revered building in America. But he was right in stating that its combination of dignity, harmony, and utility made it a fit embodiment of the highest traits of the Republic. Thornton's classic design, stamped with the approval of Washington and Jefferson, so happily expressed the majesty of our democracy that most of the state capitols reared since have echoed its lines. This, we may say, is the spirit of America in stone.

Doubtless everyone, gazing at the Dome completed amid rigors of war, or entering the Rotunda where Lincoln, Garfield, McKinley, Kennedy, and Unknown Soldiers lay in state, thinks first of the august penumbra of history that enwraps the structure.

On its steps nearly all the Presidents since Jackson have been inaugurated. This is where Lafayette was welcomed as symbol of one epochal alliance, and Winston Churchill as partner in another. In the Old House Chamber, now Statuary Hall, every visitor must feel moved at the spot where John Quincy Adams sank under his mortal stroke in 1848. Who can enter the President's Room without reflecting, "Here it was that Lincoln

# of Resounding Deeds

indomitably defied his Senate leaders by refusing to sign the radical Wade-Davis bill upon Reconstruction."

Some rooms are heavy with history. In the Old Senate Chamber, occupied from Buchanan's day by the Supreme Court, Webster replied to Hayne. The treaty closing the Mexican War was ratified. Clay and Calhoun battled over the Compromise of 1850. And great Court decisions from the legal tender cases under Grant to the NIRA case under Roosevelt in 1935 were handed down.

Many of the transactions witnessed by Capitol walls still lift the hearts of men. Here Adams battled for the right of petition, and when one opponent offered a resolution for his censure as a traitor, he demanded that the clerk read the first paragraph of the Declaration of Independence as his sufficient answer. Here, as the House was trying Sam Houston for assaulting a fellow Member, Drayton of South Carolina declared that if freedom of discussion were ever restrained, the pillars of the Constitution would fall.

Here, in the middle of one war, Tom Corwin had the courage to proclaim that if he were a Mexican, he would welcome American invaders with bloody hands to hospitable graves; and just before our entry in another, Robert M. La Follette, Sr., halted the armed-ship bill amid a hurricane of denunciation. Here, when Andrew Johnson was placed on trial, a little knot of determined men vindicated the demands of justice and the authority of the Presidency.

We can assert that the Capitol has heard eloquence equaling that of any parliament on earth; that it has written into law such immortal charters of idealism as the Fourteenth Amendment; and that in its foreign-aid bills it has enacted the most generous measures known to history. But our proudest boast is that no Capitol in the world has done more to safeguard free democratic debate, the privileges of minorities, and the fundamental civil liberties of man.

We would do an injustice to the spirit of the Capitol, however, if we emphasized merely the great men and dramatic events associated with it. The value of democratic government lies mainly in the place it gives to ordinary aspiring men and women. Since 1800 the Capitol has been the scene of grim, hard work by many thousands of conscientious legislators and their aides who have thought little of public fame, but much of the honest accomplishment of their tasks. We too often treat these servants, toiling early and late, as a matter of course.

If the stars were visible only once in a thousand years, wrote Emerson, we should await the spectacle with breathless interest; but our legislators, like the stars, are visible all the time, and hence are little noted unless of special magnitude. The Capitol is History; it is the Major Symbol of the Nation, full of minor symbols; but above all it is a Mighty Engine, tended and kept throbbing by the indefatigable efforts of a select assemblage which represents far more of our national strengths than of our national weaknesses.

ALLAN NEVINS
(1890-1971)

On its hilltop, outlined sharply against the sky, stands the Nation's Capitol,

The Meaning of the Capitol

By LONNELLE AIKMAN

LIKE A VISION in fantasy, the great white Dome of the United States Capitol rises above the trees at the end of converging avenues in Washington. Floodlit by night or cameo-cut against azure skies, it reminds Americans of classroom prints and pledges of allegiance, of high school Civics I, commemorative stamps—and a procession of domed and columned statehouses repeating the classic national profile all across the land. No other building, not even the White House, is so intimately linked with the lives

citadel of democracy epitomized in Alexander Hamilton's "Here, sir, the people govern."

of all the people of the United States. It stands at the heart of our system of representative government. It is a focal point of American ideals of freedom and opportunity. It is proof—in stone, marble, and partisan debate—of the capacity of citizens to join in the adventures and satisfactions of governing themselves.

Here our elected representatives make the laws we live by under our Constitution, which begins, "We, the people . . . in order to form a more perfect Union, establish justice . . . provide for the common defense, promote the general welfare. . . ." Here voices raised in legislative debate echo accents of 50 states. They speak of the conflicting interests of city, factory, and farm—of seaboard, plain, and the mountain regions in a far-flung Nation. Then the votes are counted, and all voices merge into the majority that can speak as one for the United States.

There is a phrase for this democratic process. High above Congress, it is incised on the base of the Statue of Freedom that crowns the Dome. Taken from the Great Seal of the United States, it reads *"E Pluribus Unum"*—"Out of Many, One."

Such symbolism pervades the Capitol. It was built into the walls, stone by stone, as the "Congress House" kept pace with the expanding Nation. It is inherent in the dignity of today's structure, and in the architectural balance between the two wings.

Symbolic themes turn up, too, in structural and decorative details bequeathed by dedicated architects and artists who labored on the Capitol. From pride in New World products, for instance, came the Indian-corn and tobacco-leaf designs chosen to ornament columns in the original Senate wing.

"This Capital [the column head with the corn-ear motif] . . . obtained me more applause from Members of Congress," Architect Benjamin Latrobe wrote President Thomas Jefferson, "than all the Works of Magnitude, of difficulty & of splendor that surround them."

Paintings and murals displayed throughout the building highlight events of the founding, expansion, and development of the United States. Statues and portraits of the men who took part in these struggles and achievements—soldiers, statesmen, scholars, and inventors—line the marble corridors and look out from the columned walls.

T O THE MILLIONS of sightseers who annually trudge the Capitol's immense distances, the whole effect is one of kaleidoscopic variety. Indeed, the panorama of so many ideas and objects might float off into abstractions or break up into fragments were it not that the exhibits, together, evoke the story of the United States as a nation.

It is this unifying element in our past that makes the home of Congress a tangible link between the states, recalling what Abraham Lincoln termed the "mystic chords of memory" shared by all Americans. In the Civil War, when critics complained of the cost of continuing construction, Lincoln himself cited the symbol of symbols.

"If people see the Capitol going on," a caller reported his saying, "it is a sign we intend the Union shall go on."

All three branches of the Government have had close associations with the Capitol since its first small wing was completed in 1800. For 134 years it sheltered the United States Supreme Court as well as the Congress. Here most of our Presidents have been inaugurated, beginning with Thomas Jefferson, who in 1801 strolled over from his nearby boardinghouse to take the oath of office.

FATEFUL MOMENT *and dramatic action link Nation and history within the Capitol's marbled halls. Here statesmen tread, strong wills clash, laws pass—today a nuclear-tinged issue, in the past, a Compro-*

mise of 1850. That event saw Henry Clay, aged and ill, plead to the Senate for a middle road in the North-South split over allowing slavery's spread to western lands. Daniel Webster (front row, second from left) listened, then put Union before self to speak for the compromise —and lost all chance at the Presidency. Vice President Millard Fillmore presides here, his elbow above John C. Calhoun. William Seward, Secretary of State under Lincoln, leans on the desk at right.

LINCOLN'S INAUGURAL *in 1861 took place beneath hoists and scaffolds on the Capitol Dome. Bayonets glinted as the President-elect spoke of possible civil war and reminded "dissatisfied fellow countrymen" of his oath to "preserve, protect and defend" the Constitution. Chief Justice Taney then administered that oath in a scene (below) sketched by artist Thomas Nast.*

Most Presidents since Jackson have been sworn in on the Capitol steps.

Highest-ranking officials of our three-way system come together in the House Chamber whenever the Chief Executive delivers his State of the Union Message to a Joint Session of Congress, usually attended by the Justices of the Supreme Court.

More American leaders have dreamed, planned, worked, and argued in the Capitol than in any other single spot in the United States. Twenty-two of our Presidents served in this building as Representatives or Senators, or both, before achieving the Nation's highest office. Two of them, John Quincy Adams and Andrew Johnson, returned after-

ward to the House and Senate respectively.

"My election as President . . . was not half so gratifying to my inmost soul," Adams confided to his diary in 1830, after winning a seat in the Twenty-second Congress.

To Johnson, his welcome back to the Senate in 1875, after the humiliation of his impeachment trial as President in that same room, was even greater balm for wounded pride. In a chamber filled with rejoicing friends and disconcerted enemies, he received congratulations and flowers, magnanimously shaking hands with men who had voted for his conviction.

Some of the most dramatic events in our political life took place at the Capitol, beginning with the vote by the House giving Jefferson the Presidency over Aaron Burr after the electoral tie of February 1801.

During the first 60 years, Congress fought out the "great debates" over issues that split the country: Foreign-trade restrictions and protective tariffs in the early 1800's; bank legislation of Jackson's time; slave- and free-state contests marking long shadows of the coming Civil War.

On a grieving April day in 1865, Lincoln's funeral cortege moved from the White House toward the Capitol that lately had flamed with gaslight celebration on Richmond's fall. In the Rotunda, the body remained on view as thousands filed through the building to pay their last respects.

There, before a Joint Session of Congress, on April 2, 1917, Woodrow Wilson asked for a declaration of war against Germany. "The world," he said, "must be made safe for democracy." And Franklin Delano Roosevelt, before a similar session, opened another Presidential war message with the words, "Yesterday, December 7, 1941—a date which will live in infamy. . . ."

Soldiers, statesmen, poets—many others—have spoken here. On a February day in 1962, a modest, thoughtful man stood before Congress assembled to hear a report that would have seemed sheer lunacy not so long before. The speaker was Lt. Col. John H. Glenn, Jr.; the subject, his experience as the first American astronaut to whirl in space around the earth.

"We have only begun," President John F. Kennedy told Congress in his January 1963 State of the Union Message. "Upon our achievement of greater vitality and strength . . . hangs our fate and future in the world."

Ten months later an assassin's bullet had cut down America's youngest elected President. At the Capitol, his successor—former Vice President and President of the Senate Lyndon B. Johnson—voiced a pledge:

"We will continue," Johnson said, ". . . that we may fulfill the destiny that history has set for us."

Along with crises and high moments, the Capitol witnessed the central miracle of a nation in the making—the enactment of long-range legislation that pulled a continent together, coordinated its natural wealth, and helped root in its soil what we call the American way of life.

In fact, action by Congress established all but a very few of the departments and agencies of the Government; all owe their continued existence to the sanction of the people's representatives, whose far-reaching and complex responsibilities today can be measured by the size and activities of the Capitol building itself.

It towers 287 feet $5^1/_2$ inches, from East Front base to the top of the Statue of Freedom. It is 350 feet wide and more than 751 feet long. Its floor area covers $16^1/_2$ acres. Its 540 rooms hum with the sound and movement of committee hearings, administrative and maintenance work, and a thousand other operations devoted to the perennial consideration of legislation.

How this huge, labyrinthine building became the center and symbol of a nation that has existed for only two centuries is an American success story all the more fascinating because it began in a swamp and under the most unlikely circumstances.

ROTUNDA VISITORS *gather in the great circular hall beneath the Capitol Dome. The cordoned passage provides an unobstructed walkway for Senators and Representatives. The large oil paintings by John Trumbull depict scenes from the American Revolution: (from left) the presentation of the Declaration of Independence, the surrender of General John Burgoyne at Saratoga and of Lord Cornwallis at Yorktown.*

PENSIVE LINCOLN *dwarfs a tiny admirer. The work of Vinnie Ream (left), the statue stands at the west entrance of the Rotunda. Lincoln let her sketch him in the White House when he learned that she was poor.*

15

A Building
and a Nation
Grow

N OT EVERYONE was pleased, in 1790, when Congress
decided to establish the young Republic's permanent
seat on the banks of the Potomac River instead of ac-
cepting one of a dozen other sites offered.

"A howling, malarious, wilderness," some called the area
chosen. "The Indian place . . . in the woods on the Potomac," said one disgusted official.

But the decision had been made, and much could be said for
it. Washington, District of Columbia—marked off by, and
named for, the first President—was near the midpoint of the
long stretch of states. It lay close to the thriving centers of
Georgetown and Alexandria, accessible to overland and wa-
ter transport. "It is a beautiful spot, capable of any improve-
ment,"said Mrs. John Adams when she first saw her brief
home as the wife of the second President, ". . . the more I
view it the more I am delighted with it."

Few realized it then, but the embryo settlement also was favored by the vision of a city planner on the grand scale. Pierre
Charles L'Enfant, French-born engineer who had served under General Washington in the Revolution, laid out a city
whose broad avenues and sweeping circles anticipated the
needs of the future metropolis.

On a June morning in 1791, President Washington and
L'Enfant made a horseback inspection of the Federal District's wooded and swampy site. L'Enfant had prepared a
map and a report on the city's proposed features, including
the home of Congress and the "presidential palace," linked
by a broad green mall.

"I could discover no one [situation]," L'Enfant wrote in
his report, "so advantageously to greet the congressional

PRESIDENT WASHINGTON, *wearing sash, collar, and
apron of the Masonic order, lays the cornerstone
for the Capitol on September 18, 1793. Dismantling
in 1959 at the building's East Front failed to
uncover the original stone. Its approximate location
is marked by a plaque beside the Old Supreme Court
entrance. The marble-headed gavel and silver trowel
Washington used still exist; they have figured in
later stone-setting ceremonies at the Capitol, the
Washington Monument, and other public structures.*

1793

PAINTING BY ALLYN COX

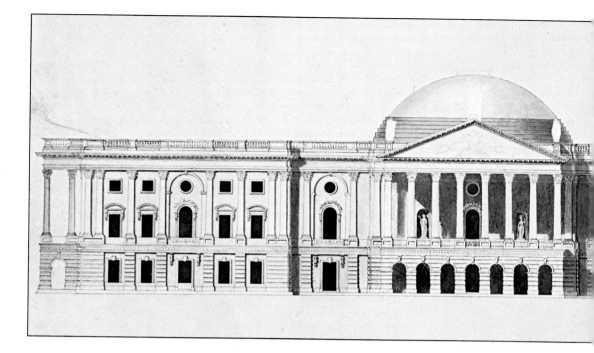

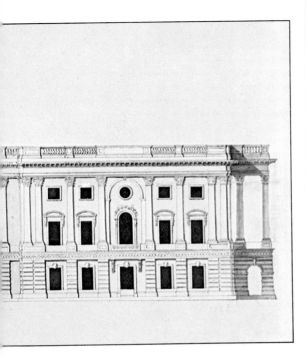

LOW-DOMED BUILDING *won for Dr. William Thornton a 1792 competition for a Capitol design. His prize: $500 and a city lot. Washington praised the plan for its "Grandeur, Simplicity and Convenience." The original drawing was lost; this one dates back to the mid-1790's.*

CAPITOL DESIGN *by Stephen Hallet placed second in the contest. He was named to oversee construction on Thornton's draft, but, ambitious, sought to put in ideas from his own. Commissioners discharged him in 1794.*

OUTSIZE WEATHERCOCK *topped the Capitol building proposed by James Diamond, of Maryland. Other sketches submitted in the rivalry had equally impossible details or odd proportions; few trained architects then existed in the United States.*

WILLIAM THORNTON —*physician, painter, and inventor—turned amateur architect to enter and win the competition to design the U. S. Capitol. Born in 1759 on a tiny island near Tortola in the West Indies, he had moved to the United States only in 1787, after studying medicine in Edinburgh and living in Paris.*

The deadline for Capitol entries was just six days off when Thornton asked for and received permission to send his design in late. The plan that finally arrived "captivated the eyes and judgment of all," Secretary of State Thomas Jefferson noted.

As one of three federal commissioners, Thornton clashed with Hallet and other experienced architects during the Capitol's construction. He became head of the Patent Office in 1802. A story credits his pleas to a British officer with saving that building from being burned in the War of 1812.

Thornton died in 1828.

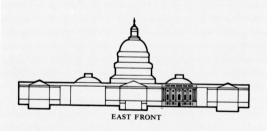

EAST FRONT

BOXLIKE WING of the old Capitol, first to be completed, served Senate, House, and Supreme Court. This watercolor, done in 1800, shows the wing's location in today's building. Sandstone used in the construction came from a Virginia quarry.

building as is that on the west end of Jenkins heights. . . ." It stands, he added in the felicitous, oft-quoted phrase, "as a pedestal waiting for a monument."

To obtain a suitable design for their monument, the District Commissioners announced a Capitol competition, offering the winner $500 and a city lot. The contest was advertised in newspapers of the young country, but professional architects were few, and none of the entries proved satisfactory. Some were ludicrous—one design was crowned by a monstrous weathercock with wings spread wide.

At this crucial moment, a versatile young man named William Thornton (physician, portrait painter, steamboat experimenter, and amateur architect) gained permission to submit a belated design.

When his plan arrived, it "captivated the eyes and judgment of all," said another tal-

ented amateur architect—Thomas Jefferson, then Secretary of State.

"Grandeur, Simplicity and Convenience appear to be so well combined in this plan . . ." George Washington wrote in a letter of recommendation to the District Commissioners, "that I have no doubt of its meeting with . . . approbation from you."

By September 18, 1793, Dr. Thornton's design for a stately building with two wings joined by a domed center had been selected and modified. Troublesome construction problems had been resolved, and the time had come to lay the Capitol's cornerstone.

The day's program involved elaborate Masonic ceremonies, a common practice then, with roots going back to the link between medieval stonemasons and the order. As President, war hero, and Acting Grand Master of Maryland's Grand Lodge, Washington had the lead role, supported by a uniformed and decorated cast from the Alexandria Volunteer Artillery and Masonic lodges of Maryland, Virginia, and the District. A parade began with the President's arrival on

SLOOPS EDGE *Philadelphia wharves as the Government moves to Washington from its last temporary capital in 1800.*

the Virginia shore of the "Grand River Patowmack," crossed to the Maryland side, and moved on to the President's Square, collecting additions at each meeting place.

"The procession marched two abreast," an observer reported in the September 25th issue of the *Alexandria Gazette,* in Virginia, "in the greatest solemn dignity, with music playing, drums beating, colours flying and spectators rejoicing."

Skirting the "great Serbonian Bog" that was then Pennsylvania Avenue, the marchers followed a new post road, broke ranks to step from stone to stone or teeter over a single log across Tiber Creek at the foot of Capitol Hill, and then proceeded to the hilltop building site.

There, Washington, wearing a Masonic

apron reputed to be "the handiwork of Mrs. General Lafayette," conducted the ceremony with a marble-headed gavel and a silver trowel. In laying the cornerstone, he placed it on a silver plate marking the date as the 13th year of American independence, the first year of his second term, and the year of Masonry 5793.

The cornerstone's exact site remains uncertain, though it may be in the southeast corner of the Capitol's original north wing.

"The ceremony ended in prayer, Masonic chanting Honours, and a fifteen volley from the Artillery," the *Alexandria Gazette* informed its readers. "The whole company retired to an extensive booth, where an ox of 500 pounds' weight was barbequed, of which the company generally partook, with

STONEMASONS *working on the Capitol chiseled a personal trademark on the stones they dressed. Most marks lie hidden in the construction or under plaster. These mason's marks show in a stairwell of the old House wing.*

JAMES HOBAN *gained a footnote in history by his prize-winning plans for the "President's Palace"—the White House—in 1792. But he also had a part in shaping the Capitol. Born in Ireland in 1758, he trained as an artisan and architect and emigrated to the United States after the Revolution. He lived in South Carolina and designed, among other buildings, the State House, burned during the Civil War. Winning the White House contest brought Hoban an appointment to superintend construction. A year later the Capitol became his responsibility, too. With but one break, he was Capitol Superintendent until 1802, though his assistant Stephen Hallet for a time took rather free rein. Hoban was active in Government building until his death in 1831.*

© 1958 JAMES HOBAN ALEXANDER

Claimed by Great Britain and United States.

Claimed by Great Britain and United States.

To Massachusetts

Area disputed by Great Britain, Spain and United States.

LOUISIANA PURCHASE

VT.

N.H.

NEW YORK   MASS.

R. I.

CONN.

PENNA.

N.J

INDIANA TERRITORY   OHIO   MD.   DEL.

SPANISH

VIRGINIA

KENTUCKY

TENNESSEE   N. CAROLINA

Ceded by Georgia 1802.   S. CAROLINA

MISSISSIPPI TERRITORY   GEORGIA

SPANISH

Area claimed by United States as part of purchase.

■ States
■ Territories
□ Unorganized, U.S.
□ Foreign

LEWIS AND CLARK, *on funds voted by Congress, began their journey to the Pacific in 1804. "Crossing the Bitterroots" portrays the explorers struggling along an Indian trail through the mountains. The first official party to cross the Louisiana Purchase after its acquisition from the French, the expedition confirmed the immense value of the land. An unexpected bargain offered by Napoleon, the $15,000,000 Purchase nearly doubled the Nation's size. The Senate approved the treaty 24 to 7.*

BENJAMIN HENRY LATROBE *took over construction of the Capitol on his appointment as Surveyor of Public Buildings in 1803. An English architect, he was born in 1764 and came to the United States in 1796. The Capitol's exterior design was already set, so he poured out his genius on the interior. Hiring sculptors from abroad, he put them to work executing ideas that won acclaim, including corn and tobacco motifs on columns (below). Latrobe had the task of repairing the Capitol, burned by the British in 1814, but resigned in 1817. He died in 1820.*

every abundance of other recreation."

It was a brave beginning, but troubles were already brewing.

One of the difficulties was the rivalry between Dr. Thornton, the official Architect of the Capitol, and a series of professional architects who wished to alter the prize-winning design.

Etienne Sulpice Hallet, or Stephen Hallet, as Americans simplified the French name, was the first to come to grief over this issue. Hallet's disappointment in having been rated second best in the original competition complicated the conflict. By the end of 1794, Hallet—in charge of construction at the Capitol—had been dismissed, and Thornton appointed to be one of the three District Commissioners, with over-all authority to back up his own ideas.

MEANTIME, the meager sale of lots in the straggling village failed to finance the public buildings, as had been hoped. The Commissioners were forced to borrow money on loans guaranteed by Congress. Skilled workmen, tools, and materials needed to build the Capitol proved hard to find.

Yet somehow the Congress House progressed. The first, or north, wing was completed under the general direction of the superintendent of construction, James Hoban, who designed and also directed the building of the "President's Palace"—the White House. Except for details, the wing was ready to receive the legislators by the autumn of 1800, when the Government had moved, bag and baggage, from its last temporary seat at Philadelphia.

In the columned Senate Chamber, under the intent gaze of spectators, President John Adams addressed the first Joint Session in the building on November 22, 1800. He wore the formal coat, knee breeches, and powdered hair of the time, and his words reflected the importance of the occasion. Not until Woodrow Wilson—on April 8, 1913—would another President appear in person to address the Congress.

"I congratulate the people of the United States on the assembling of Congress at the permanent seat of their government," President Adams said, "and I congratulate you, gentlemen, on the prospect of a residence

not to be changed. . . . May this Territory be the residence of virtue and happiness! In this city may that piety and virtue, that wisdom and magnanimity, that constancy and self-government, which adorned the great character whose name it bears, be forever held in veneration!"

Both the congratulations and the hopes must have echoed hollowly to the lawmakers as they prepared to settle down in the near-wilderness of the District of Columbia during that first winter of 1800.

"I do not perceive," Secretary of the Treasury Oliver Wolcott wrote his wife in Connecticut, "how the members of Congress can possibly secure lodgings, unless they will consent to live like Scholars in a college or Monks in a monastery, crowded ten or twenty in one house, and utterly secluded from Society."

The situation was hardly better at the Capitol itself, where the 32-member Senate,

WEST FRONT

LATROBE'S 1810 MODIFICATION *(top) of the exterior in William Thornton's original plan joined House and Senate wings with a colonnaded central portico. The tinted section in the sketch depicts the House wing occupied in 1807.*

106-man House, Supreme Court, Circuit Court, and Library of Congress would soon share one modest rectangular building.

Officials and clerks, however, could already see prospects for expansion in the partially laid foundations of the Capitol's central section and south wing protruding from the barren, stone-cluttered hilltop. And soon began a game of musical chairs, played by these august branches of Government as they exchanged old quarters for new in a forever changing and growing building.

The Representatives moved first (1801), into a one-story, oval-shaped hall—appropriately nicknamed the "Oven"—erected temporarily on the south-wing site. The Oven was razed in 1804, and House Members returned to their earlier quarters on the west side of the north wing. There they met for three more years while their own chamber rose where the Oven had stood.

The architect now in charge of the Capitol was Benjamin Henry Latrobe, appointed by President Jefferson in 1803.

As had Washington, Jefferson took a keen personal interest in the building's development, even to dictating many of its details. He particularly admired Latrobe's finished

SHOUTING HEADLINES in Boston's Columbian Centinel of June 24, 1812, announce the step urged on Congress by fiery young "War Hawks" in its ranks. They called war "the only means of redress" for interference with American trade, impressment of American seamen, and other acts by Great Britain. At the war's end, the Capitol where they spoke stood gutted by fire.

House Chamber, with its carvings, classical columns, and visitors' gallery.

"I declared on many and all occasions," he wrote Latrobe, "that I considered you as the only person in the United States who could have executed the . . . Chamber. . . ."

UNFORTUNATELY, though all agreed that the new room was magnificent in appearance, its acoustics proved far from satisfactory. Virginia Representative John Randolph of Roanoke summed up the verdict when he called it "handsome and fit for anything but the use intended."

While the House hung red-baize draperies behind Corinthian columns in an effort to muffle resounding echoes, the Senate grappled with its own brand of construction and moving-day problems.

Besides stopping leaks and patching cracks that threatened the north wing with premature decay, Latrobe rebuilt the east part of the wing, thus creating two separate rooms—one for the Senate and one for the Supreme Court a floor below.

During the renovation, displaced Senators occupied quarters on the wing's west side, then in January 1810 took over the

"**BATTLE OF LAKE ERIE,**" *a painting by William H. Powell, hangs in the east stairway of the Senate wing. It depicts 28-year-old Oliver Hazard Perry transferring the colors from his battered flagship, the* Lawrence, *to the* Niagara *in the 1813 engagement. Victorious, Perry sent his now famous dispatch: "We have met the enemy and they are ours. . . ."*

BRITISH TROOPS, *ordered to "destroy and lay waste," set fire to public buildings in Washington on August 24, 1814. The act incensed Americans and shamed many Britons. "Cossacks spared Paris, but we spared not the Capitol of America," one newspaper said. This sketch appeared in London in 1815.*

REAR ADM. SIR GEORGE COCKBURN *took part in firing the Capitol. Reportedly, he stood on the House Speaker's chair and asked, "Shall this harbor of Yankee democracy be burned?"*

BURNED-OUT CAPITOL *stood stark after a rainstorm checked the flames. Piled furniture, books from the Library of Congress, and tar barrels made tinder for the blaze. Latrobe replaced the charred interior with marble, brick, and stone.*

TREASURY REPORT *survived the fire. Handwriting on its flyleaf says Admiral Cockburn took it from the Capitol and gave it to his brother. A dealer presented it to the Library of Congress in 1940.*

29

MONROE'S INAUGURAL
*outdoors settled a dispute
over whether to sit
on the Senate's "fine
red chairs" or the "plain
democratic" ones of the
House. His open-air oath-
taking—later a tradition—
occurred at the "Brick Capitol" (left). The building
housed Congress during
1815-19 repairs to the
burned quarters. A prison
during the Civil War, it
stood where the Supreme
Court Building now rises.*

30

top part of their old chamber. In turn, the Supreme Court, then made up of seven members, transferred its sessions to the ground-floor level.

Presiding was Chief Justice John Marshall, whose brilliant career would build the Court's prestige as arbiter of the Constitution, and lay a firm legal foundation for the legislative powers of Congress.

Hardly a dozen years had passed since the Government's move to Washington, but already its leaders could look back with pride. They had built two wings of a Capitol planned to accommodate more than 500 future lawmakers. And they had made enough national history there to indicate that the building's scope was not excessive.

In 1803 Congress ratified Jefferson's vast Louisiana Purchase—though not without lively discussion as to whether it violated the Constitution. Congress voted funds for the Lewis and Clark Expedition, which revealed a new world of dazzling promise and sobering responsibility to men struggling in Washington to unify a string of independent-minded coastal states. And it appropriated money to strengthen the infant United States Navy for action against Barbary pirates preying on Mediterranean shipping.

Then came a day in November 1805 when a mission from the Bey of Tunis arrived in the village by the Potomac. The Senate received the Tunisian Ambassador in its chamber, where that turbaned envoy expressed bewilderment at the spectacle of ordinary men being allowed to speak on the conduct of their government.

Less picturesque, but more significant, was the establishment by Congress in 1800 of a reference library. From the first $5,000 provided to stock the Capitol's one-room Library of Congress would come a world-renowned institution that now occupies three huge buildings, including the James Madison Memorial Building completed in 1980. These structures hold more than 80 million items in collections of books, newspapers, periodicals, manuscripts, films, maps, and works of drama, music, and art.

"There is . . . no subject to which a Member of Congress may not have occasion to refer," Jefferson wrote in an observation even more applicable today.

But first the young Republic faced the War of 1812—and ordeal by fire—to determine whether either Capitol or Library, or, indeed, the Nation itself, would have a future.

Congress declared war against Great Britain on June 18, 1812, after long and bitter debates between "War Hawks" and peace proponents over neutral rights, British impressment of American seamen, western lands, and other issues that created bad feeling between the two countries.

For many months after fighting began, most of the action took place far from Washington. Then, in the late summer of 1814, a British squadron under Rear Adm. Sir George Cockburn landed soldiers and marines near Benedict on Maryland's Patuxent shore. Brushing aside American forces hurriedly gathered at Bladensburg, the invaders captured Washington on August 24 and set fire to most of its public buildings.

INDIGNANT PATRIOTS later claimed that Cockburn himself had led a detachment of troops into the House Chamber. They said he took over the Speaker's chair and put the rhetorical question, "Shall this harbor of Yankee democracy be burned?" The motion carried with a roar of "ayes."

The men ignited piles of flammable materials—chairs, desks, and books—in both House and Senate wings. Interiors were gutted, exteriors scarred and blackened, and the wooden passageway between the two buildings was destroyed.

Destruction would probably have been total, except for a rainstorm that swept the city that night. The next day brought a violent windstorm. Its force destroyed houses, killed 30 British soldiers, and blew cannon off their mounts. Together with an accidental gunpowder explosion and a false rumor that American troops were gathering to retake Washington, the chain of disasters so shook British confidence that the redcoats moved out, never to return.

Amid the clamor of Members demanding the Government's transfer to another city, the homeless Congress met that fall in the Patent Office Building, formerly Sam Blodget's hotel—the only Government office structure to escape burning.

From late 1815 to 1819, Congressional

sessions were held in a new building hastily erected by a group of private citizens and rented cheaply to Congress as an inducement to stay on. This building, long known as the Brick Capitol, stood on the site of what is now the United States Supreme Court Building. There, on March 4, 1817, James Monroe took the Presidential oath in Washington's first outdoor inaugural.

The ceremony—"grand, animating and impressive"—was held outside, instead of in the House Chamber, to settle a deadlock on whether to use the Representatives' "plain democratic chairs" or transfer the "fine red chairs" from the Senate.

Meanwhile, the rebuilding of the Capitol proceeded under the direction of Architect Latrobe, who had spent the war years away on projects ranging from designing Mississippi steamboats to planning waterworks for New Orleans.

On his recall in 1815, Latrobe found "the devastation . . . dreadful . . . a most magnificent ruin." Setting resolutely to work, he strengthened as well as restored both wings, using sandstone and marble, brick and stone. He enlarged and beautified the Senate Chamber, and redesigned the House Chamber into the semicircular shape we see today as Statuary Hall.

SCARLET CURTAINS *in the Old House Chamber hung as much for utility as for decoration—to muffle annoying echoes. Samuel F. B. Morse painted this night session of the House in 1822. Visitors now see the area as Statuary Hall.*

Done before Morse turned from easel to telegraph experiments, the painting shows an attendant lighting the lowered chandelier. In 1847 gas lamps came, electricity in 1885. Morse faithfully reproduced House details and recorded Members' likenesses by individual sittings.

LAFAYETTE'S PORTRAIT, *a gift to the U. S. by the artist, Ary Scheffer, has hung in the House since 1825.*

But Latrobe, too, suffered from the occupational hazard of Capitol architects—disagreement with his boss, the Commissioner of Public Buildings. He resigned in 1817 to make way for able Boston architect Charles Bulfinch, the first American-born citizen to receive the appointment.

To Bulfinch goes the credit for completing the Capitol as Thornton and Latrobe had planned it. He worked out remaining structural details of Senate and House Chambers in time for Congress to move back on December 6, 1819. And Bulfinch carried through the building's long-planned central portion, including its east and west fronts,

33

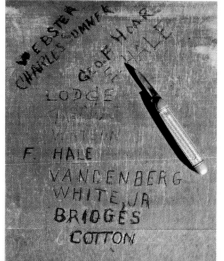

"LIBERTY AND UNION, *now and forever, one and inseparable!" booms Daniel Webster. His reply countered the states' rights stand of South Carolina's Senator Hayne. The date: 1830. This painting of the Old Senate Chamber by G.P.A. Healy hangs in Boston's Faneuil Hall.*

NAMES CARVED *in a drawer of Webster's desk note other Senators who have occupied the great orator's seat.*

CITY OF BOSTON

and a central Rotunda covered by a low copper-sheathed dome.

The cornerstone for the Capitol's center section was laid on August 24, 1818, four years to the day after the British conflagration. By October 1824, the Rotunda interior was complete and ready for the city to hold a gala reception to honor a visiting dignitary and old friend—the Marquis de Lafayette. Fashionable Washington—eager to shake the hand of the French general and statesman who had helped create the Nation— jammed the great circular hall.

In December, Congress officially received the Revolutionary hero, making him the first foreign visitor to speak before a Joint Meeting. Lafayette was aging now, but with charm undiminished by the years. To a remark made by Henry Clay, Speaker of the House, that he stood "in the midst of posterity," he replied that, on the contrary, he stood in the midst of his friends.

From the 1820's to the eve of the Civil War, the Capitol was the stage for momentous and tragic events—sometimes for scenes not far from comic opera. It was the

35

BUCOLIC WASHINGTON *in 1833 spreads around a domed Capitol and the White House. The flag marks the Navy Yard. Traditionally, no nearby buildings may rise above the Capitol.*

WEST FRONT

BULFINCH'S DOME *and central addition gave Congress's home this look from 1825 to 1856. City planner L'Enfant called its hill site "a pedestal waiting for a monument."*

era of leisurely oratory, filled with learned classical allusions, and on occasion with insults that led Congressional opponents to uphold their honor on the dueling field.

It was an age of chivalry, when the gentlemen of the House and Senate welcomed visiting ladies to the floors of their respective halls, or, seeing their guests sitting for hours in hot and crowded galleries, would hand up refreshments of fruit fastened to the ends of long sticks.

But most of all it was a time of struggle and dissension, a period when sectional rivalries strained the bonds between the states and the national Government.

The arena of test and decision was the United States Congress. Here opposing

CHARLES BULFINCH *became the first American-born architect to have charge of construction at the Capitol. Boston-born in 1763, he received a Harvard education, followed by years of practical experience in building construction and wide study of architecture abroad. When Latrobe resigned in 1817, Bulfinch was appointed to succeed him on work at the Capitol.*

There the able Bostonian mainly carried out plans set down by predecessors, although he did modify Latrobe's grandiose design for the West Front into the more pleasing lines it has today. To him goes much of the credit for keeping construction of the Capitol moving toward completion.

Bulfinch left Washington in 1830, a year after his position as Architect was abolished. Not until 1851 was there a successor—or need for one— except on a temporary basis. Bulfinch died in 1844.

leaders wooed followers and votes in verbal combats on such crucial subjects as the tariff, states' rights, and conflicting interests of various sections of the country.

Within this same short time span, the Capitol also saw much to nourish America's increasing sense of national pride and "manifest destiny." In 1823, Congress heard the bold Monroe Doctrine proclaimed, warning Europe's rulers against intervention in this hemisphere. Congress voted for annexation of Texas in 1845, and the next year for war with Mexico and a treaty with Great Britain to settle the dispute over the far Northwest. By the end of 1848, these events had brought the Southwest, California, and the Oregon Territory under the United States flag. In

January of that year, as a bonus, gold was discovered in California.

Now the sectional question hung heavy with threat. In the North-South battle to block or extend the spread of slavery to the West, which side would win? Or would both lose in the breakup of the Union?

For four decades the divisive rivalry called into play the talents and energies of some of the most dynamic men who ever sat in Congress. Three stood out as giants.

Spellbinder Henry Clay of Kentucky won his brightest laurels for his role in slavery-compromise bills of 1820 and 1850 that gave the South a temporary middle ground between secession and submission—and the North years of economic growth that made victory possible in the fratricidal war.

John C. Calhoun, of South Carolina, fought more often against Clay than with him, and ended his political career with a tragic plea for concessions from the North.

COLONNADED WALLS *of the Old Senate Chamber once resounded to orations by John C. Calhoun, Henry Clay, and Daniel Webster. In lighter moments, gentlemen on the floor passed up refreshments by sticks to friends in the stuffy galleries.*

In a mezzotint (below), the hall appears as it did in 1842. Engraver Thomas Doney made the print by peopling the gallery and chamber with individual daguerreotypes of Senators and other noted persons. A present-day artist added color.

For the Bicentennial the Old Senate Chamber was restored to look as it did when last occupied by the Senate in 1859 (right).

ORIGINAL FURNISHINGS *of the restored chamber include the Vice President's curved desk and lamp (upper dais), Rembrandt Peale's portrait of Washington, and reproductions of the 64 desks and the curved gallery with its bronzed railing. The gilded eagle (above) perches as it did when the Supreme Court occupied the room for 75 years.*

41

Yet Calhoun's parliamentary genius, mastery of logic, and personal integrity earned for this champion of rights of a minority the permanent respect of his country.

Last of the triumvirate was Daniel Webster of Massachusetts. The most compelling orator America has produced, he poured his heart and thunderous eloquence into the struggle to preserve the Union. In his "Seventh of March" speech, he dramatically pleaded for Senate passage of Clay's 1850 compromise, but at high cost to himself. By daring to repudiate not only his Free Soil followers, but also his own pledge to oppose extension of slavery—in any place, at any time—Webster was denounced by friends and lost his last chance of winning enough support to achieve what had been his greatest ambition, the Presidency.

Throughout the long tumult, states continued to join the Union, population soared, and Congress grew. In 1850, the 62 Senators and 232 Representatives were beginning to feel crowded. Ironically, the drive for more space was spearheaded by Senator Jefferson Davis, whose later fame as President of the Confederate States has overshadowed his earlier career.

Congress in September 1850 appropriated $100,000 to begin work on "ample accommodations for the two houses of Congress," an enlargement that would reduce the Capitol's original wings to the role of links between the additions and the central Rotunda. President Millard Fillmore, authorized to select both the design and the architect, chose respected Philadelphia architect Thomas U. Walter to execute the design for the Capitol's extension.

The building's third cornerstone laying took place on July 4, 1851. It was an unqualified success, free "from all untoward occurrences," reported Washington's popular newspaper, the *National Intelligencer*. "The day was ushered in by salutes of artillery from different points of the city, and as the glorious sun gilded our tallest spires, and shed a lustre on the dome of the Capitol, it was welcomed by a display of National Flags and the ringing of bells from the various churches and engine houses."

President Fillmore and the Grand Master of the Masonic fraternity, B. B. French, laid the stone in elaborate civil and Masonic ceremonies. But the chief event for which the crowd had gathered from far and near was the dedication address by the old master, Daniel Webster, now Secretary of State.

The most frequently quoted paragraph from Webster's two-hour speech was also part of his own handwritten statement buried inside the cornerstone.

"If therefore," his deep, melodic voice rang out over the Capitol's stilled east plaza, "it shall be hereafter the will of God that this structure shall fall from its base, that its foundation be upturned, and this deposit brought to the eyes of men, be it then known that, on this day, the Union of the United States stands firm; that their constitution still exists unimpaired, and with all its original usefulness and glory. . . ."

MORSE'S TELEGRAPH *taps its historic "What hath God wrought!" from the Supreme Court Chamber, May 24, 1844. Annie Ellsworth gives the inventor the message to be sent—a privilege earned when she brought him word, a year earlier, that Congress had voted funds to build a line from Washington to Baltimore. Witnesses to its test included Henry Clay, standing by Dolley Madison in the background.*

The Smithsonian Institution owns this key (right) used by Morse.

Work on the massive additions to the Capitol went forward as fast as possible, but Architect Walter faced many problems, including the usual conflicts over authority, trouble in obtaining materials, and a fire in 1851 that made it necessary to reconstruct the area housing the Library of Congress.

NEITHER WING was fully complete when House and Senate moved in—the House for its first session in the south wing, December 16, 1857, and the Senate in the north wing, January 4, 1859. The legislative halls were equipped with paneled walls, arabesque decorations, and intricate glass-and-iron skylights—even with newfangled gas lighting. The House substituted upholstered settees for its desks in 1859, but only briefly. Members voted to bring desks back

the following year—and continued to use them until 1913.

Meantime, considering the precarious political situation of the 1850's, the Capitol's lavish furnishings and plans for the future seemed decidedly incongruous.

As the decade closed, the clash of wills in Congress reflected the country's rising tensions. Abolitionists and slavery diehards jammed the shiny new galleries, tossing out leaflets and hissing or cheering the impassioned speakers.

"Every man on the floor of both Houses is armed with a revolver," observed one Senator. When a Member accidentally dropped his weapon during a bitter eight-week struggle to elect a Speaker of the House, the uproar threatened to turn into mob violence.

Yet when secession came, and, one by

PIONEERS STRUGGLE *across a rugged divide in this mural at the west staircase of the House wing. Titled "Westward the Course of Empire Takes Its Way," it was painted by Emanuel Leutze in 1862.*

Plains from Wyoming to New Mexico still show ruts cut by lurching wagons as waves of immigrants rolled west. They followed the lure of land and gold, and they peopled a burgeoning nation.

EXPLODING GROWTH *saw the Nation fulfill a "manifest destiny" to stretch from sea to sea. Between 1840 and 1860, the population nearly doubled, to 31 million. The acquisition of land forced Congress to debate whether new states should be slave or free. The Compromise of 1850 quieted the issue for a time; the Kansas-Nebraska Act rekindled sectional furies that led to war.*

1840

States

U.S. Territories

Unorganized, U.S.

Foreign

1860

SOLDIERS LOLL *in the Rotunda in 1861. The Capitol served as barracks
in the early months of the war, then as a hospital for the wounded.
Men called their quarters the "Big Tent." Here canvas shields
Rotunda paintings; a scaffold rises for construction of the Dome.*

one, the Southerners bade their colleagues goodbye, the scenes were often stiff with dignity and poignant with pent-up emotion. No speech was more dramatic than the appeal to his colleagues, on January 10, 1861, by the Senator from Mississippi—gaunt, courtly Jefferson Davis.

Like Calhoun, Davis pleaded for peace. He had tried to avert war, he told the Senators and the presiding officer, Vice President Breckinridge of Kentucky, who also would soon be joining the Confederate side. But if peace was not to be, said Davis, "then Mississippi's gallant sons will stand like a wall of fire around their State; and I go hence, not in hostility to you, but in love and allegiance to her. . . ."

In the gallery sat Davis's beautiful dark-haired wife, Varina. "We felt blood in the air," she would write later, "and mourned in

CAPITOL VAULTS *became storehouses for flour, beef, and pork when Washington feared siege at the war's onset. From stockpiles in arched passages, barrels skidded down planked steps to improvised bakeries. Basement committee rooms, bricked into ovens, made bread for Army forts and batteries ringing the city.*

47

HOISTED COLUMN *swings into place on the portico linking the old and new House wings. Men at right of the pillar probably are Jefferson Davis, a Mississippi Senator when this 1860 photograph was made, and Thomas U. Walter, Capitol Architect.*

CANVAS SHIELDS *men dressing columns. The House wing lacks porticoes finished in 1867.*

TIERED DOME *rises atop the Capitol during Civil War years. Lincoln called construction "a sign we intend the Union shall go on." The cast-iron Dome, designed by Walter and weighing nine million pounds, replaced the low Bulfinch structure dismantled in the photograph at left. The tower inside the Dome helped lift materials into place from the Capitol grounds.*

CART-SLUNG COLUMN *of iron, one of 36 in the Dome, arrives for placement. Maryland marble went into the Capitol extension's 100 other columns—each cut from a single block of stone.*

49

EAST FRONT

DOME AND WINGS *added to the Capitol in the 1850's and 1860's brought the structure to the form so familiar today. This 1871 lithograph, hand colored, pictures it dominating a tree-dotted city from atop Jenkins Hill. The Washington Monument, incorrectly shown with capstone and hexagonal base, actually was not completed until 1884.*

secret over the severance of tender ties both of relationship and friendship . . . we could even guess at the end."

Southbound Congressmen were well on their way home when President-elect Abraham Lincoln arrived on February 23, early and unannounced, in the Washington railway station. The curtain was rising on the most fateful years the Nation had yet faced.

At the Capitol on Inauguration Day, a tall, gangling figure stood on the wind-raked stand built over the East Front steps. There had been rumors of a plot to blow up the platform. Riflemen watched from the windows behind the speaker. Below him glinted the fixed bayonets of a line of soldiers.

Adjusting his steel-rimmed spectacles, Lincoln looked out on a sea of faces, not all friendly, since Washington was filled with Southern sympathizers. To these people, and those in the South, Lincoln addressed his famous appeal for conciliation:

50

"In *your* hands, my dissatisfied fellow countrymen, and not in *mine*, is the momentous issue of civil war. . . . We are not enemies, but friends. We must not be enemies. Though passion may have strained, it must not break our bonds of affection."

But the firmness in Lincoln's inaugural speech discouraged any hope that a compromise with secession would be possible. "I hold," he said, "that in contemplation of universal law, and of the Constitution, the Union of these States is perpetual. . . . no State, upon its own mere motion, can lawfully get out of the Union. . . . The power confided to me, will be used to hold, occupy, and possess the property, and places belonging to the government. . . ."

A month and eight days later, Confederate guns fired on Fort Sumter. For the rest of the war, the Capitol at Washington would be the Union's stronghold and symbol. The "Old Brick Capitol," across the way, would

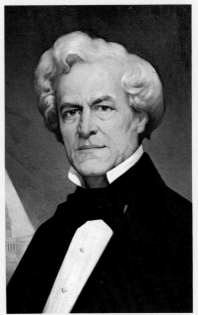

THOMAS USTICK WALTER guided construction during one of the Capitol's most important periods of change. Named Architect of the Capitol Extension by President Fillmore in 1851, he served until 1865—eventful years that saw the building grow almost threefold.

Walter's father and grandfather were masons, and the Philadelphia-born youth himself became a master bricklayer while studying in an architect's office. He set up shop for himself in 1830. When a contest for enlarging the Capitol opened in 1850, Walter entered.

Construction of the Capitol's wings began immediately after Walter's appointment. He ran into many problems, including conflicts over authority. The Capitol Dome he built is considered a notable engineering feat.

Born in 1804, he died in 1887. His portrait by Francisco Pausas, based on a Mathew Brady photograph, shows him as Capitol Architect.

51

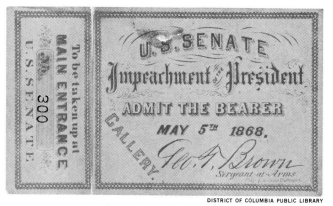

THIS COVETED TICKET — *the Senate gallery had fewer than 800 seats—brought admission to the 1868 impeachment trial of President Andrew Johnson. Colors changed each day of the trial.*

CROWDED SENATE CHAMBER *hears Thaddeus Stevens read the House message of impeachment. Stevens led the attempt to punish Johnson for his opposition to Congress. Sitting as a court, the Senate failed by a single vote to convict. Had impeachment succeeded, the Constitution's system of checks and balances might have given way to a parliamentary type of government.*

PRESIDENT JOHNSON, *by his White House desk, accepts impeachment summons from the Senate Sergeant at Arms. As did Lincoln, Johnson favored leniency toward the South; he irked Congress by his stubbornness on Reconstruction and other Administration issues.*

CARRIED IN A CHAIR, *Thaddeus Stevens enters the Capitol during the impeachment trial. Contemporary accounts called him "an infirm old man . . . upheld only by an iron will." He died a few months later.*

52

become a prison, housing for a while two famed Confederate spies, seductive Rose Greenhow and spirited Belle Boyd.

Congress was not in session when war broke out. Immediately the War Department took over the marble spaces of the newly enlarged Capitol as barracks for Northern regiments marching into the city on the President's call for 75,000 state militia. The boys termed their quarters the "Big Tent," and boasted of portrait-hung parlors, comfortable sofas, and desks for writing letters home. For a time 3,000 soldiers slept in the building, from the Rotunda and legislative chambers to hall niches and airy nooks up near the unfinished, open Dome. Mealtime found lines of hungry men waiting to cook rations of bacon, biscuits, and coffee at furnaces lighted in the basement.

The furnaces sparked an idea. Basement committee rooms were converted into a bakery that included room-size ovens lined with fire bricks. Flour was commandeered from the city's mills. The aroma of fresh-baked bread drifted about the Capitol as Army bakers turned out enough extra loaves to feed soldiers in forts and batteries springing up around Washington.

By the next autumn the cheerful bustle and youthful high jinks of what had been romantically pictured as a short, gallant war had given way to harsher realities. The Capitol, like lesser buildings, became an emergency hospital. Set up in its historic halls, chambers, and Rotunda were 1,500 cots, on which lay the sick and wounded streaming back from the battlefields of Second Manassas and Antietam.

Among the city's doctors—and a sprinkling of nurses stirred by the example of Dorothea Dix and America's future Red Cross founder, Clara Barton—moved a gentle, bearded man. Walt Whitman, poet and humanitarian, spent most of his spare time during the war in Army hospitals, dispensing small gifts and large doses of cheer.

"The hurt and wounded I pacify with soothing hand," he would write later in a poem of remembrance. "I sit by the restless all the dark night, some are so young."

With the return of Congress, following the patients' transfer to other hospitals, the Capitol became the sounding board of fears and suspicions that fevered the air of the nerve-wracked city. Accusations rang out in legislative chambers. A Joint Committee on the Conduct of the War investigated charges of incompetence and conspiracy. Not even the President's home escaped the pointing finger. Gossips whispered that Mary Lincoln was a spy in the White House, seeking to protect relatives who were fighting on the side of the Confederates.

One morning at a secret session of investigating Senators, the towering figure of Abraham Lincoln suddenly appeared at the committee table. One of those present recalled years later that Lincoln's eyes were filled with "an almost unhuman sadness."

The President told the astonished group that he had come of his own volition, "to say that I, of my own knowledge, know that it is untrue that any of my family holds treasonable communication with the enemy."

"By tacit consent, no word being spoken," the narrator of the incident reported, "the committee dropped all consideration of the rumors that the wife of the President was betraying the Union."

DESPITE THE WAR, some work was done on the Capitol extension. Construction of a vastly enlarged Dome—authorized by Congress in 1855 to replace the one dwarfed by the new wings—continued.

Designed by Architect Walter, the big Dome is a masterpiece of 19th-century engineering skill. It has outer and inner cast-iron shells, trussed to withstand the strains of contraction and expansion. Intricately girded and bolted together, it weighs nearly nine million pounds. Between the shells winds a narrow staircase of 183 steps.

To raise the heavy iron parts to their lofty places, construction superintendent M. C. Meigs built a scaffold tower from the floor of the Rotunda up through the Dome. It served as a base for the hoisting devices used to lift the materials on the outside.

The great bronze goddess that crowns the Dome's lantern structure was the work of an outstanding American sculptor, Thomas Crawford. He referred to her as "Freedom triumphant," and shaped her as a classical figure, with one hand on a sword, the other holding a wreath and resting on a shield.

Her feathered headdress has led many to believe that the statue represents Pocahontas or some other Indian. Actually, Crawford had designed the headdress as a liberty cap, after those worn by Rome's emancipated slaves. He substituted a helmet with eagle head and Indian feathers to meet the objections of Jefferson Davis, future President of the Confederacy, who had charge of Capitol construction as Secretary of War from 1853 to 1857.

Modeled in Crawford's Rome studio, the statue's plaster cast was imperiled by a leaky ship, heavy gales, and other hazards on an eight months' journey to the United States. By October 1862, the bronze form was cast at Clark Mills' foundry in Washington and the city's residents had an opportunity to inspect the $19^1/_2$-foot figure temporarily

OLD LIBRARY OF CONGRESS *quarters in the Capitol abound with ornate metalwork. As the Library's collection outstripped shelf space, piles of books accumulated on the floor, as seen in this 1867 photograph. By 1890, bagged items leaned against columns of stacked books. The need for more space prompted a drive for the Library's own building, finished in 1897. The Library today is among the world's largest; its 78 million items echo Jefferson's remark that "there . . . is no subject to which a Member of Congress may not have occasion to refer."*

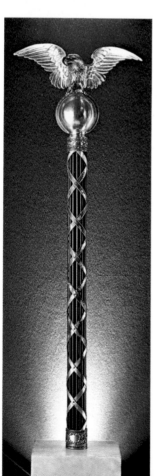

CARRYING THE MACE, *symbol of authority in the House, the Sergeant at Arms rounds up Members for a quorum. This 1881 artist's conception appeared in* Leslie's *weekly. Actually, the mace rests on a stand beside the rostrum except in rare cases when displayed before an unruly Member to restore order. Its position at the rostrum tells whether the House is in "committee" or "session" —an aid for determining the number needed for a quorum.*

The first House mace was destroyed when the British burned the Capitol. A painted wood facsimile substituted until 1841, when a silver-and-ebony copy of the original was made (left). Its eagle and globe surmount rods representing the first 13 states. Length is 46 inches.

OATH-TAKING CEREMONY *of Vice President Theodore Roosevelt, March 4, 1901, finds President-elect William McKinley (center) among the spectators. Until 1937 Vice Presidents took the oath in the Senate Chamber; later, they usually stood on the Capitol steps.*

displayed on the grounds of the Capitol.

Finally, at the appointed hour of 12 noon, December 2, 1863, the giant head of Freedom—last of the statue's five sections—was raised and bolted into place.

The United States flag, bearing 35 stars for all the states, Northern and Southern, fluttered overhead. Spectators cheered. Capitol Hill's field battery boomed a 35-gun salute, one for each state. In turn, a dozen Union forts rimming Washington roared back a pledge of 35-gun responses.

The Capitol was crowned, but it was not yet complete. The east portico of the new Senate wing would be finished in the fall of 1864, but several more years would pass before its north and west entrances were in place. By 1867 all the porticoes of the Repre-

sentatives' wing also had been built, but it was 1916 before the sculptured east pediment for the House was at last unveiled.

Today, the Capitol includes a major addition—a $32\frac{1}{2}$-foot eastward extension of the central area. This substantial enlargement won the support in 1955 of the late Sam Rayburn, Member of the House for 48 years and its Speaker for 17, who steered bills containing the proposal past Congressional hurdles.

President Eisenhower laid the extension's cornerstone on July 4, 1959. A Masonic ceremony followed. Work went forward under the direction of the late Capitol Architect J. George Stewart. The new front was in place just in time for President John F. Kennedy's inauguration on January 20, 1961.

Nearly a century earlier Walter had called

such construction "an architectural necessity" to balance the added wings and Dome. Succeeding Capitol architects recommended the expansion against an outcry that no change should be made in America's treasured historic monument.

The protests rose sharply when Congress in 1956 and again in 1958 took action in favor of the controversial construction. Yet many of its severest critics now agree that the new East Front has added beauty and much-needed working space in which to carry on the ever-increasing legislative needs of the growing country.

Pushing the building's midsection forward eliminated the impression that the huge Dome overhung the central portico. The builders preserved, as interior supports, the walls that stood when General Lafayette visited the Rotunda. At the same time they replaced the old sandstone front with one of durable marble, every detail of hand-carved decoration faithfully copied from the crumbling originals.

Sandblasters laboriously took 32 layers of paint from the ironwork of the Dome. The replacement coats—requiring 1,750 gallons —were toned to match the marble of the wings, cleaned to pristine whiteness for the first time since 1862.

INSIDE, the Capitol gained two and a half acres of space spread over five floors. Brought into being were 102 rooms, including individual offices, committee and reception rooms, dining rooms, kitchens, and entrance foyers.

There are additional elevators and—by no means the least of the useful innovations— private corridors that link the north and south wings. For the first time, Members of the Congress can walk between Senate and House Chambers and various offices without having to elbow their way through crowds of sightseers.

But will the Capitol ever be finished? For years opposing factions in the Senate and House debated the question of what to do about the deteriorating West Front.

One group proposed that it be extended as was the East Front to provide more space for offices and other facilities. The other group wanted to repair and reinforce the crumbling

sandstone walls of the West Front built from 1793 to 1826, the only visible part of the original sandstone exterior.

A decision to repair and reinforce the West Front was finally voted by Congress in July 1983; preservation and restoration began soon after. In the autumn of 1987, painting and other finishing touches concluded work on this historic and spectacular section of the Capitol.

Since 1908, six huge office buildings,

three for the House and three for the Senate, have been built nearby to help fill the need for office space, committee hearings, and other activities of Congress.

The House structures were named for Speakers Joseph Cannon, Nicholas Longworth, and Sam Rayburn. The Senate trio honors Senators Richard Russell, Everett Dirksen, and Philip Hart. The Hart building alone added an estimated one million square feet of floor space.

HUSHED JOINT SESSION *in February 1917 hears President Woodrow Wilson announce the severance of diplomatic relations with Germany. Four years earlier he had set a precedent by becoming the first Chief Executive to address Congress in person since John Adams did so in 1800. Beneath the flag, Vice President Thomas Marshall and Speaker Champ Clark (in light suit) preside.*

59

HUGO H. HARPER

PRESIDENT COOLIDGE *bestows the Medal of Honor on Charles A. Lindbergh for his historic flight across the Atlantic. Popularly called the "Congressional" medal, this highest of the Nation's decorations is awarded by the President in the name of Congress for "gallantry and intrepidity at the risk of life." Others in the 1928 picture at the White House are Speaker Nicholas Longworth, Vice President Charles G. Dawes, and Secretary of War Dwight Davis.*

LAUREL WREATH *and goddess Minerva embellish the Army's Medal of Honor. Reverse here bears Lindbergh citation. Navy version differs slightly in design.*

The Rayburn Building, most recent of the House office structures, was completed in 1965. A massive edifice of marble and granite, it became the backdrop—in the spring and summer of 1974—for one of the great dramas in American history.

The setting was Room 2141; the characters, 36 men and two women, members of the House Committee on the Judiciary. Their unrehearsed role was to weigh the evidence and vote on articles of impeachment accusing President Nixon, under the Constitution, of "high crimes and misdemeanors."

The climax to the drama came near the end of July, with the final debates and votes televised live for the public. As millions of viewers watched and listened throughout the United States, and by satellite abroad, the committee, with bipartisan support, overwhelmingly passed three articles of impeachment to be submitted for the consideration of the full House.

If the House had approved the articles, as was predicted by many who followed the proceedings, the Senate would then have been required to conduct its second impeachment trial of a President

BLINDFOLDED *with cloth taken from a chair in Independence Hall, Secretary of War Henry L. Stimson begins the 1940 draft—first enacted by Congress in peacetime. President Roosevelt read the number Stimson drew, 158. The same bowl did duty in the 1917 wartime draft.*

HARRIS & EWING

UNITED PRESS INTERNATIONAL

of the United States. Instead, Mr. Nixon avoided the ordeal that Andrew Johnson had suffered 106 years before by resigning his office—the first Chief Executive in American history to do so.

The House Judiciary Committee thus became the most famous of such investigative bodies in modern times. But there are also hundreds of other committees and subcommittees of Congress that meet regularly on vital national and international issues in the offices and suites scattered throughout the Capitol and related office buildings.

In the light of the enormous amount and variety of business that Congress must now deal with, it seems strange to recall that no supplementary areas were provided outside the Capitol until 1908, when the first House Office Building was opened. Before that, Members sometimes rented their own offices in downtown Washington.

EACH NEW OFFICE BUILDING has brought an enlargement of the Capitol complex, now totaling more than 200 acres. The stately park around the Capitol itself holds an unusually fine collection of American and foreign trees—as well as a variety of shrubs and flowers. Cherry trees, dogwoods, azaleas, and tulips flourish here.

The Capitol's landscaping was carried out mostly in the mid-1870's by Frederick Law Olmsted, designer of New York's Central Park. In those days, certain areas at the Capitol served for croquet games, and others for egg rolling by children at Easter. But perhaps the sharpest reminder of a vanished era appears in a routine report of 1877. Plants and bushes, it said, had been damaged by stray cows of the neighborhood.

Since such incidents, the Capitol has both reflected and affected the changes that have swept the country and the world. It has seen Congress grow to 100 Senators and 435 Representatives, plus the nonvoting Resident Commissioner from Puerto Rico and delegates of the Virgin Islands, Guam, American Samoa, and the District of Columbia. So steadily did population expansion boost House membership that Congress in 1911 limited the number to the presently voting 435.

The U. S. Congress belies the saying that

GEORGE M. WHITE, *first professional architect selected since 1865, was appointed Architect of the Capitol in 1971. His credits include construction of the James Madison Memorial Building of the Library of Congress, the design and construction of the Philip A. Hart Senate Office Building, and restoration of the Old Supreme Court and Old Senate Chambers in the Capitol. White holds advanced degrees in engineering, business administration, and law. He is a fellow and former vice president of the American Institute of Architects.*

ATTENTION FOCUSES *on the West Front of the Capitol. When its central section—more than 160 years old—began to crack and crumble, one group in Congress favored extending the facade as a remedy. But another group's views won out and set in motion work to strengthen and preserve the old sandstone walls.*

HIGHEST FINAL TRIBUTE *of the Nation: The Unknown Serviceman of the Vietnam Era lies in state in the Capitol Rotunda. At the ceremony, attended by government dignitaries, military officials, veterans, and other notable guests, President Reagan (center, in background with his wife, Nancy) placed a wreath beside the casket. "We may not know his name, but we know his courage," the President said in eulogy. Only 26 men— among them nine Presidents—have lain in state on the black catafalque that first held the body of Abraham Lincoln.*

those who make a nation's songs mold its character. In laws passed here, a knowledgeable student can trace the course of modern America's economic, political, and social development.

Between the lines of Reconstruction legislation, he can feel the passions and furies of bitter adjustments. Thumbing through the homestead acts, the reader can almost hear the "whoop and holler" with which each wave of westbound pioneers took over the Government's freely offered acres for cattle-raising, farming, and timberlands.

The rise of big industry and high finance, based on seemingly endless raw materials and subject to boom-and-bust speculation, brought regulation of interstate commerce, food, and drugs. In time came restrictions on investments, trusts, and monopolies, and laws to conserve the country's natural

65

resources and to protect the environment.

President McKinley's war message to Congress launched the Spanish-American War in 1898 and marked U. S. participation in world politics on an ever-increasing scale.

Twentieth-century Americans can look back on legislation that has transformed the Nation and their own lives. Though we don't always realize it, our daily talk, newspapers, and TV often reflect changes brought about by Congressional bills and the broad principles of Constitutional amendments.

The process began with the Bill of Rights—the ten original amendments. The first and most familiar article guarantees freedom of religion, of speech, of the press, and the right of the people peaceably to assemble and to petition the government.

Other amendments adopted since 1791 include the right to vote (1870) regardless of "race, color, or previous condition of servitude"; the income-tax amendment of 1913; woman suffrage in 1920; prohibition in 1919, and its repeal in 1933.

Among still other life-touching legislation are social security, civil rights and medical-benefits bills, and currently, still-debated laws designed to cope with federal deficits versus social and military obligations.

All this, and more, has been built into the U. S. Capitol and is part of what visitors may see and sense in the home of Congress.

SENATE AND HOUSE meet in Joint Session on January 31, 1990, to hear President George Bush deliver his State of the Union Address. "America stands at the center of a widening circle of freedom—today, tomorrow, and into the next century," he declared. The Constitution requires the Chief Executive to "give to the Congress Information of the State of the Union," a message traditionally presented annually by the President in the House Chamber. Mr. Bush stands at the intermediary dais. Behind him sit Vice President Dan Quayle (left) and Speaker of the House Thomas S. Foley. Supreme Court Justices, Cabinet Members, and the Joint Chiefs of Staff fill temporary seats in front of the rostrum. Senators and Representatives occupy the remaining seats. Eleven Presidents since Woodrow Wilson have called special Joint Sessions to discuss urgent issues. Wilson's 20 appearances before Congress remain a record.

UNITED PRESS INTERNATIONAL

STATESMEN, AUTHORS, ASTRONAUTS—*all have addressed Congress: Winston Churchill after Pearl Harbor; Carl Sandburg honoring Lincoln; Frank Borman on behalf of American prisoners of war in Vietnam.*

Exploring Today's Capitol

STAND ON the Capitol plaza, facing the monumental east steps. There you occupy a spot from which Americans have witnessed most Presidential inaugurals since Andrew Jackson brought the ceremony out to cheering followers in 1829.

Architect Bulfinch's central portico had just been completed then. Spilling out from the plaza before it was a milling crowd of bankers, workmen, housewives, town merchants, and visiting frontiersmen, some of whom had walked far to see the triumph of the "People's President." Between the portico's towering columns and on its stone steps stood Washington's great and their ladies. "Scarlet, purple, blue, yellow, white draperies and waving plumes of every kind and colour . . . had a fine effect," wrote a social commentator of the times.

On these steps during the Civil War, Lincoln spoke the compassionate words, "With malice toward none; with charity for all. . . ." There Franklin Roosevelt told a Nation trying to lift itself out of depression that "the only thing we have to fear is fear itself." And John F. Kennedy said, "Ask not what your country can do for you—ask what you can do for your country."

Starting with Andrew Jackson, 27 elected Presidents took the oath of office at the East Front. On January 20, 1981, this precedent was broken when President Ronald Reagan and his Vice President, George Bush, were inaugurated at the West Front.

Before 1937, Vice Presidents were sworn in within the Senate Chamber. Since then, with two exceptions, they have participated in the inaugural ceremonies with the incoming Presidents. The exceptions were Gerald Ford and Nelson Rockefeller. These nonelected Vice Presidents took the oath in the House and Senate Chamber, respectively. The law allows the President, with confirmation by Congress, to appoint the person to fill a vacancy in the Vice Presidency.

President Reagan's second inaugural, in 1985, was unusual in several ways. Since the official January 20 date fell on Sunday, he was sworn into office on that day, with the public proceedings set for the following day.

The Sunday ceremony took place near the marble Grand Staircase in the White House. It was an affair witnessed only by top officials, close personal friends and relatives, plus a small pool of reporters. The event marked the fourth double inaugural; the others were for Hayes, Wilson, and Eisenhower. When the official date fell on Sunday in 1821 and 1849, the ceremony for Monroe and for Taylor was postponed to Monday— the only occasions when this solution was used for the Sunday inaugural problem.

The well-laid plans for the 1985 events were further complicated by devastating weather. A cold spell that dropped the temperature to zero—with a wind chill as low as minus 50°F—forced the swearing-in ceremony to be moved from the open West Front into the Capitol Rotunda. It also prompted the cancellation of the customary parade on Pennsylvania Avenue.

The indoor ceremony on Monday, a historic first for the Rotunda, was performed before a standing-room-only audience that included selected citizens and some of the Nation's most prestigious officials.

The traditional inauguration, long staged for the public every four years at the East Front, has a symbolic backdrop that recalls the early days of the Republic.

Carved on the East Portico's pediment above the assembled dignitaries stand three classical female forms, representing America flanked by Justice and Hope.

The theme was inspired by President John Quincy Adams, who pictured Hope as "a

WASHINGTON IN BRONZE *stands against the monumental background of the Dome's interior. Figures in the overhead painting—an allegorical glorification of the first President—were drawn as much as 15 feet high to seem life-size from the Rotunda floor 180 feet below.*

BRONZE DOORS, *modeled by Randolph Rogers in the 1850's, lead to the Rotunda. Rep. J. J. Pickle explains to staff members that the doors depict events in the life of Columbus. Below, a visitor studies another bronze door, the entrance to the East Portico of the House wing. Designed by Thomas Crawford, the scene portrays George Washington in 1783 bidding farewell to his officers in New York.*

Scriptural Image.'' Her support by an anchor indicated, he wrote, ''that this Hope relies upon a Supreme Disposer of events.'' President Adams rejected a proposal to include Hercules as smacking ''too much of the heathen mythology.''

Look beyond Adams's pediment and you see the great Dome as immobile. But is it? The iron structure moves imperceptibly at the whim of the weather. Scientists once demonstrated that sections of the double-walled, nine-million-pound Dome may expand and contract as much as four inches on days of temperature extremes.

Walk across the main East Portico, and you pass the statues of War and Peace designed by Luigi Persico, the same Italian artist who carried out the pediment adornment. Then pause before the massive bronze doors leading to the Capitol Rotunda.

These gleaming ten-ton portals portray events from the life of Columbus. Designed in high relief by American sculptor Randolph Rogers, they follow techniques used by Ghiberti and other Italian masters.

Rogers modeled his doors in Rome during the 1850's and had them cast in the Royal Bavarian Foundry of Munich. When installed, the doors opened into the corridor between Statuary Hall and the new House wing. They were hung at the Rotunda entrance in 1871.

Pass through the doors and into the Rotunda. You're now at the heart of the Capitol, and at the hub of streets that lead to it from north, south, east, and west. Here is another case of built-in symbolism, going back to L'Enfant—whose plan put the Capitol at the center of his grid of city streets.

The Capitol's huge circular hall—nearly 100 feet across and more than 180 feet high—also is the heart of the building's historic art displays. From here a maze of rooms and corridors extends into Senate and House wings. Many are filled with sculptures and paintings collected over the years by purchase, gift, or commissions to artists.

On encircling walls of the Rotunda hang eight immense oil paintings. Four depict happenings of the fledgling days of discovery and colonization. One, ''The Baptism of

Pocahontas" by John Chapman, attracts viewers who have heard of the six-toed Indian that the artist included among the spectators. Some 200 years after the baptism, one descendant of Pocahontas—the brilliant and erratic John Randolph of Roanoke—sat in Congress as Representative and Senator.

The other four works are priceless links with the American Revolution. Sketched while the leaders were alive, they portray the presentation of the Declaration of Independence, the surrender of Gen. John Burgoyne at Saratoga and of Lord Cornwallis at Yorktown, and General Washington resigning his commission at Annapolis.

Their creator, John Trumbull, had served briefly as an aide to Washington. He knew many of his subjects and traveled far to obtain likenesses. He painted John Adams in London, when the future U. S. President was Minister to England. In Paris, amid rumblings of the French Revolution, Trumbull made a portrait of Thomas Jefferson, then Minister to the royal government.

"I have been in this capital of dissipation and nonsense near six weeks," Trumbull wrote his brother Jonathan in 1788, "for the

HEROIC FIGURES *vividly appear in this close-up of the Dome's "Apotheosis of Washington." To cover the 4,664 square feet of concave surface, Constantino Brumidi worked in fresco— paint applied to newly troweled plaster. Brumidi, almost 60, finished his masterpiece in 11 months, signing it in 1865. A conservation project completed in 1988 removed the grime of decades to reveal the fresco's original beauty and three-dimensional details.*

Forms in the inner circle represent the 13 original states and the Union; Washington sits between Liberty and laureled Victory. Outer groups—clockwise from sword-wielding Freedom— symbolize arts and sciences, the sea, commerce, mechanics, and agriculture.

GODS AND MORTALS *mingle in the Dome's fresco. Sandaled Mercury offers a bag of gold to Robert Morris, "financier of the* *Revolution." Vulcan rests his foot on a cannon. Ceres rides a reaper as Young America, wearing liberty cap, stands near.*

Bearded Neptune and Aphrodite, holding the Atlantic cable, rise from the sea. Wise Minerva speaks to Benjamin Franklin, S.F.B.

Morse, and Robert Fulton. Armed Freedom —Brumidi's young wife was the model— triumphs over Tyranny and Kingly Power.

SCULPTURED SHARPNESS *in wall-flat fresco emblazons the Nation's history on the Rotunda frieze. Brumidi began it, but died while painting "Penn's Treaty with the Indians." Using Brumidi's sketches, Filippo Costaggini finished the panel and eight others, including "Colonization of New England" (right).*

purpose of getting the portraits of the French Officers who were at York Town, and have happily been . . . successfull."

Such human stories, repeated by successive generations of Americans, are like family anecdotes told of favorite ancestors. They breathe spirit into the sculpture around the Rotunda's sweeping walls.

One, the tall, commanding figure of Washington, is a bronze copy of Jean-Antoine Houdon's true-to-life statue displayed in the State Capitol at Richmond, Virginia.

On either side of Washington stand Jefferson and Hamilton, who made a political bargain that gave the Federal Capital its Potomac site.

Treasury Secretary Alexander Hamilton was seeking legislation to have the national Government assume state debts incurred during the Revolution. Encountering Jefferson near the President's house when New York was the seat of government, Hamilton persuaded the Virginian to use his influence with Southern legislators to win votes for the debt assumption. In return, the Southerners were offered Northern support in placing the Capital in a more central location.

The agreement bore fruit in the act of 1790 that established the Government's residence beside the Potomac. But it brought gibes at the time. One newspaper wrote that "Miss Assumption," beguiled by the promises of "Mr. Residence," had given birth to the child "Potowmacus."

Memories of the War of 1812 cling to the slim bronze statue of Gen. Andrew Jackson, seen in the dashing uniform and cape he wore as the victor of the Battle of New Orleans. Considering the speed of today's communications, it is ironic to recall that neither side in the battle knew peace had already been signed.

As President in 1835, "Old Hickory" almost lost his life near the spot where his statue now stands. He had attended funeral *(Continued on page 83)*

CONSTANTINO BRUMIDI *fled from Rome in his late 40's to escape political persecution. He had been born there in 1805, studied at the Academy of Arts, and gained repute by restoring Vatican frescoes. Coming to the United States, he spent a quarter-century—for pay averaging $3,200 a year—working "to make beautiful the Capitol of the one country on earth in which there is liberty." He slipped from a scaffold in 1879 while painting the Rotunda frieze, but managed to grasp the platform and hang 58 feet above the floor until help came. The shock, however, hurried his death a few months later. Mathew Brady photographed him with brush and palette in the 1860's.*

VISITORS SHRINK *to doll size when seen from the topmost balcony within the Dome. Once the public could climb twisting, narrow stairs to this lofty walkway. But so many persons collapsed and had to be carried down, and so much trash was tossed below, that the area was closed. Frescoed figures march in an endless band around the Rotunda's frieze. The railings just above guard the Dome's lower balcony. A camera hung from a rope across the chasm made this picture.*

TOP HATS AND BUSTLES *date tourists of 1871. By the time a visitor climbed to the cupola, said one account, "his collapsed state leaves him in no condition to appreciate" the view.*

"EMBARKATION OF THE PILGRIMS" *hangs in the Rotunda with seven other historic paintings. Artist Robert Weir shows the group praying as they set out from Holland, in 1620, for England and the New World.*

"SURRENDER OF GENERAL BURGOYNE." *Trumbull portrays British commander John Burgoyne presenting his sword in defeat to Gen. Horatio Gates after the Battle of Saratoga, turning point in the Revolutionary War.*

"SURRENDER OF LORD CORNWALLIS." *Trumbull portrays Cornwallis's brigadier, Charles O'Hara, tendering the British surrender to Washington's mounted emissary, Benjamin Lincoln, at Yorktown, October 19, 1781.*

"GENERAL GEORGE WASHINGTON RESIGNING HIS COMMISSION," *by Trumbull, shows the Commander in Chief of the Army before Congress at Annapolis, on December 23, 1783. Martha Washington watches from the balcony.*

STATUARY HALL, *restored in time for the Bicentennial, welcomes visitors. Using Samuel Morse's 1822 painting of the chamber (pages 32-33) as a guide, the Capitol Architect's staff refurbished the hall to look as it did when the House met here until 1857. The statue depicting "Liberty" has gazed down from her niche above the south door since the early 1800's. On the opposite wall Clio, the Muse of History (above, right), rides in a winged chariot and records passing events. Once the official clock of the House, this timepiece—attached to one of the first neoclassic sculptures to be displayed in a U. S. public building—has marked the minutes since 1819.*

services for a Member of Congress in the House Chamber, and was about to leave the Rotunda when a man stepped out from the crowd and aimed a pistol point-blank. The gun misfired. He whipped out a second hidden by his cloak. It, too, misfired in this, the first attempt to assassinate a U. S. President. The assailant was found to be insane.

Another era, the Nation's most tragic, comes to mind as you pass the stocky form of the Civil War general Ulysses S. Grant.

"I can't spare this man," Lincoln once replied to Grant's detractors. "He fights."

Today's visitors often stand quietly before a life-size marble statue of Abraham Lincoln in the Rotunda. Behind the carving lies a story, seldom told, of talented Vinnie Ream. Vinnie, 17 and shy, had begun to attract notice for her talent as a sculptor, and she longed to create a likeness of the President. A friend and adviser, Representative James Rollins of Missouri, asked Lincoln's permission for his protégée to make sketches in the White House. The President, worried by the war, paid scant attention until Rollins mentioned that the girl was poor.

"So she's young and poor, is she. Well,

MARBLE AND BRONZE FIGURES *gaze from pedestals in Statuary Hall. After serving as the House Chamber for 50 years, this room became a showcase in 1864 for statues of state notables. By law each state may place in the Capitol likenesses of two favorite citizens. Those shown here are Montana's Charles Russell, Illinois's Frances E. Willard, Virginia's Robert E. Lee, Florida's John Gorrie, Iowa's Samuel Kirkwood, and Missouri's Thomas H. Benton. A Capitol guide (below) whispers to demonstrate the hall's unusual acoustics: Her whisper can be heard clearly across the room. The tour group stands where John Quincy Adams suffered a fatal stroke on February 21, 1848.*

that's nothing agin' her," Lincoln said. "You may tell her she can come."

In half-hour sessions at the White House during the last five months of the President's life, Vinnie sketched away. She watched as he met callers and handled the burdens of the day. Later, she put it all into this marble form of a melancholy Lincoln with the pensive downward gaze.

Once Rotunda visitors saw beside the statue a giant head of Lincoln, now moved to the Capitol Crypt. The head was fashioned long after Lincoln's death by the noted sculptor Gutzon Borglum. Its powerful characterization came from a profound analysis of Lincoln "looking beyond the queer hat, bad tailoring, and boots you could not now give

away," as Borglum commented. "You will find written on his face literally all the complexity of his great nature," the sculptor continued, ". . . half smile, half sadness; half anger, half forgiveness."

In the Rotunda, a bereaved Nation has paid final tribute to 27 of its sons, including four murdered Presidents—Lincoln, Garfield, McKinley, and Kennedy.

When Kennedy's casket rested here, the lines of mourners stretched 40 blocks. Inside the Capitol, painted figures of the past looked down on ceremonies for the man who had had a special sense of history.

Henry Clay, a Member of Congress for 30 years and Secretary of State for four, was, in 1852, the first to lie in state in the Rotunda.

In the post-Civil War years, two fiery opponents of slavery, Representative Thaddeus Stevens and Senator Charles Sumner, were accorded the honor. So were Henry Wilson, Vice President under Grant, and John Logan, Union Army general and Illinois Senator, who formally initiated the Memorial Day observance in 1868.

L'Enfant's disinterred remains were brought here in 1909 in belated recognition of his genius. After L'Enfant came Adm. George Dewey of Manila fame; the Unknown Soldier of World War I; President Warren G. Harding; and Chief Justice and former President William Howard Taft, the only man to hold both offices.

Before sorrowing witnesses lay also the bodies of Gen. John J. Pershing, the commander of the American Expeditionary Forces in World War I, and of the Unknown Soldiers of World War II and Korea, both honored at the same time. In 1953, the tribute went to Senator Robert A. Taft, as it had to his father 23 years before. Since 1964, Gen. Douglas MacArthur, Senator Everett M. Dirksen, FBI Director J. Edgar Hoover, and former Presidents Herbert C. Hoover, Dwight D. Eisenhower, and Lyndon B. Johnson have all lain in state here.

In 1978, the famous black catafalque first used for Abraham Lincoln held the body of Minnesota Senator Hubert H. Humphrey, who also served as Vice President under Johnson. And in May 1984, the latest on this

special roll call was the Unknown Serviceman of the Vietnam Era.

But sadness has no part in the Rotunda's everyday activities. Mostly this room is a place of holiday crowds. "It's like St. Peter's in Rome," tourists sometimes say, looking up into the soaring Dome cut by windows through which light filters softly.

Around the Dome's eye, 180 feet above the floor, spreads a gigantic allegorical painting by the Italian artist Constantino Brumidi. The painting depicts the "Apotheosis," or glorification, of George Washington. With Washington in a sweeping circle are delicately colored figures—some 15 feet tall. They include gods and goddesses pictured as protectors of American ideals and progress.

Like most of Brumidi's work in the Capitol, the Dome decoration was done in true fresco. By this exacting technique, used by Michelangelo in the Sistine Chapel, an artist applies pigments to fresh plaster. Brumidi, high on a scaffold, had to paint fast, lest the plaster dry and force him to rework a section. To the dedicated artist, however, nothing was too difficult for his adopted country.

Born in Rome of Greek and Italian parents, Brumidi had fled his homeland in 1852 and found political refuge in the United States. He showed his gratitude by laboring from 1855 to 1880 to cover the Capitol's interior with vivid, patriotic designs.

"C. Brumidi, artist. Citizen of the U. S.," he signed his huge mural on the surrender at Yorktown, now in the House Restaurant. "My one ambition," he wrote, ". . . is that I may live long enough to make beautiful

(Continued on page 94)

CONGRESSWOMEN'S SUITE *once served as the office of the Speaker of the House. Discussing an issue are (left to right) Reps. Olympia J. Snowe, Patricia Schroeder, and Jan Meyers. On scaffolding in the House Restaurant corridor (below) noted muralist Allyn Cox surveys his work with Lonnelle Aikman, author of* We, the People. *The panel, one of a series completed in 1974, shows Washington and L'Enfant studying a plat on Jenkins Hill, site of the future Capitol.*

FREDERICK MUHLENBERG—
first to be elected Speaker, 1789.

SPEAKER'S LOBBY, located outside the House Chamber, provides an informal meeting place for Representatives. Portraits of former Speakers line the walls. Speaker of the House Thomas S. Foley (left) discusses legislation with House Minority Leader Robert H. Michel.

HENRY CLAY *molded the Speakership to its powerful role.*

HOUSE OF REPRESENTATIVES from the 101st Congress pauses for an official photograph (pages 90-91) in the House Chamber, one of the largest legislative halls in the world. The House held its first meeting in this room on December 16, 1857. Here, in its stately new quarters, the 35th Congress spent months in heated debate on the question of whether to admit Kansas as a free state or as a slave state. As House membership grew, rows of seats replaced desks; mahogany tables now provide working space for the leadership on both sides of the chamber. Above the gallery doors, 23 relief portraits of noted lawgivers from the Babylonian king Hammurabi to Thomas Jefferson remind Members of their mission. State seals border the ceiling. Behind the Speaker's rostrum Missouri marble accents the room's walnut paneling.

SAM RAYBURN *served longest— 17 years. The Speaker is second in succession to the Presidency.*

MAJORITY LEADER *Richard Gephardt (right) listens with Majority Whip William Gray and Reps. William Lehman and Edward Roybal.*

SPEAKER OF THE HOUSE *Thomas S. Foley, in highest seat of the dais (center and above), presides over the House. Leaders of the Majority Party (far left) and the Minority Party (right) use the tables in the third row of the House Chamber (above).*

MINORITY LEADER *Robert Michel (right) sits with Minority Whip Newt Gingrich and Reps. Mickey Edwards and Duncan Hunter.*

91

HOUSE READING ROOM, *located just off the Speaker's Lobby, files newspapers from the Members' hometowns. Ornate pilasters contribute to the elaborate decor. Original to the room's construction in the 1850's, the Minton-tile floor patterns are designed to resemble oriental carpets.*

THE CLERK OF THE HOUSE *(right) signs each House bill passed. Clerk Donnald K. Anderson (center) confers with Sergeant at Arms Jack Russ (left) and Deputy Clerk W. Raymond Colley. Walnut paneling enriches the House Reception Room (below), a retreat where Members can meet visitors. In a special niche stands a 5^1/$_2$-foot Sèvres vase given to the House and Senate by France in 1918.*

the Capitol of the one country on earth in which there is liberty."

Brumidi was 60 when he finished the Dome canopy, and 72 when he set up his scaffold below to begin work on his circular frieze presenting scenes from American history. He had completed six panels and was proceeding on the seventh, "Penn's Treaty with the Indians," when he suddenly lost his balance. Desperately he grabbed his scaffold and clung—58 feet from the floor—until rescuers came.

But Brumidi's working days were over. He died soon after, and Congress commissioned artist Filippo Costaggini to complete the panels. Costaggini spent eight years translating to full scale the eight small sketches left by Brumidi. Still unfinished in 1888 was a 31-foot gap, which was not filled in until 1953 by a third fresco artist, the late Allyn Cox of New York. His subjects: the

Civil War, the Spanish-American War, and the Birth of Aviation, illustrated by the Wright brothers' flight of 1903.

Approaching and entering nearby Statuary Hall, the room in which the House met from 1807 to 1857, the visitor comes upon a unique collection of 40 bronze and marble statues. Presented by various states in memory of distinguished citizens, these figures honor pioneers, missionaries, teachers, soldiers, inventors, and others who made contributions to state and country.

Here, in commanding pose, stands Ethan Allen, Vermont's Revolutionary hero who, according to tradition, demanded the surrender of Ticonderoga "in the name of the Great Jehovah and the Continental Congress."

Across the room sits a thoughtful young man examining a model of a steamboat—Robert Fulton of Pennsylvania.

Looking at the quill pen held by Charles

Carroll of Maryland, you recall a defiant patriot; he added "of Carrollton" to his signature on the Declaration of Independence so everyone could easily distinguish him.

And the name "John Gorrie M.D.," engraved on the statue contributed by Florida, identifies the ingenious doctor who patented the first ice-making machine in 1851, after experimenting with devices to cool the rooms of his fevered patients.

Some of the men commemorated in marble and bronze on pedestals lining the walls of Statuary Hall were Members of Congress who knew this room well during its half century as the House Chamber. Clay, Calhoun, and Webster sat as Representatives here. Clay served as Speaker, ruling from the throne-like chair on a platform canopied in crimson and green draperies.

The transformation of the former House Chamber into a national gallery of fame

BRONZE AND MARBLE *statues flank tobacco-leaf pillars in the Hall of Columns. By an Act of July 2, 1864, Congress invited each state to present to the Capitol two statues of citizens "worthy of national commemoration." The present collection of 95 men and women symbolizes the political, military, and cultural history of America. Shown here from left: Florida's Confederate Gen. Edmund Kirby Smith, Kansas' pioneer Governor George W. Glick, Mississippi's "Great Commoner" James Z. George, West Virginia's Senator John E. Kenna, New Jersey's "perfect soldier" Gen. Philip Kearny, and Massachusetts' Governor of the Bay Colony John Winthrop.*

began more than a century ago, after the hall had become, in the words of a legislative committee, "worse than uselessly occupied as a place of storage and traffic...."

It was "draped in cobwebs and carpeted with dust," said Representative Justin S. Morrill of Vermont in debate on the resolution to turn it into an exhibit hall.

"I look to see where Calhoun sat ... and where Clay sat and I find a woman selling oranges and root beer," remarked a colleague in supporting the measure.

As passed in July 1864, the bill cleared out the hucksters, and authorized the President to invite each state to contribute two statues of outstanding deceased citizens.

First to arrive—from Rhode Island in 1870—was a statue of Nathanael Greene, fighting Quartermaster General in the Revolution, who poured out his own fortune to supply needy soldiers. Gradually others followed, until their combined weight in the early 1930's raised fears that the whole assemblage might crash through the floor. Since then the number of statues in the room has been restricted. Others of the collection stand in the Hall of Columns on the House side and throughout the Capitol.

So far, the Capitol's roster of state notables includes 89 favorite sons and 6 favorite daughters. The first woman so honored was Frances E. Willard of Illinois, temperance leader and college president. "She possessed all the qualities of organization which have made such men as Marshall Field, Morgan, and Carnegie multimillionaires," said Illinois Senator Albert J. Hopkins when the statue was received in 1905.

All other memorials on the distaff side have been presented since 1959. Wyoming chose Esther Hobart Morris, who made history as the world's first woman justice of the peace, and who helped persuade Wyoming to become the first state to adopt woman suffrage. Minnesota immortalized Maria Sanford, educator and civic leader—called the "best-loved woman" in her state. Colorado sent a likeness of Dr. Florence Rena Sabin, the first woman member of the National Academy of Sciences. Washington State added another sculpture tribute to a woman—Mother Joseph, a Catholic nun who arrived from Canada in 1856. She and the

Sisters of Providence made valuable contributions to health care, education, and social work in the Northwest through the establishment of hospitals, schools, and orphanages.

The latest addition to the feminine ranks came in May 1985. This statue honors Montana's Jeannette Rankin, the first woman to serve in Congress. A dedicated pacifist, she made more news as a Member of the House when she voted against U. S. entry into World War I, and again as the sole dissenter to participation in World War II.

Proving that Congress can take a joke, the Capitol also exhibits a statue of Oklahoma's famous cowboy humorist, Will Rogers, who loved to josh the Members of what he called

the Washington "joke factory." When the politicians "get in that immense Hall," wrote Will, "they begin to get Serious, and it's then that they do such Amusing things."

Just outside Statuary Hall, you find the familiar, easygoing figure, cast in bronze, of the man whose homespun quips on politics brought him an opportunity to address an audience of Members of Congress and other Washington notables. At the hilarious 1933 gathering, Rogers solemnly informed Vice President John Nance Garner that he could "stay awake tonight. . . . This is one speech you haven't heard a dozen times."

Nor is Will Rogers the only cowboy to be corralled among the frock-coated statesmen

DELEGATES SIGN *the Constitution after its final drafting, September 17, 1787. The painting, acquired by Congress in 1940, hangs at the east stairway of the House wing. Artist Howard Chandler Christy worked in a Navy sail loft on the 20-by-30-foot canvas. It shows George Washington, presiding, with the Constitution's framers in Independence Hall. Alexander Hamilton talks to Benjamin Franklin (with cane). James Madison, the document's chief architect, sits at the table to Franklin's left.*

and uniformed generals in the Nation's hall of fame. Not far away stands a seven-foot statue of Montana's roving cowboy-artist Charles Marion Russell, who recorded a dying era of men and beasts in the Old West.

"You never saw one of his paintings," Rogers wrote of his friend's work, "that you couldn't tell just what the Indian, the Horse and Buffalo were thinking about."

Ceremonies in the Rotunda accompany each statue presentation. Alaska made one gift in 1971, another in 1977. In turn, the state saluted former U. S. Senator E. L. "Bob" Bartlett, called the "Architect of Alaska Statehood," and Senator Ernest Gruening, former governor and noted author.

Every state has now contributed at least one statue to the Capitol. Though Massachusetts has donated no statue of John Quincy Adams, a small bronze disk in Statuary Hall has honored his memory since 1888. The en-graved plate was set into the floor at the spot where a stroke felled Adams on February 21, 1848. He died in the Speaker's Office two days later, after 17 years of service as a highly respected Member of the House following his single term as President.

By coincidence, the Adams disk also marks the best place for guides to demonstrate the strange acoustics that so annoyed early Congressmen. Standing at the Adams plate, you can hear a whisper from across the room, though it is barely audible close by.

A second plaque was installed in the floor of Statuary Hall in 1974. This marker identifies the site of the desk used by Abraham Lincoln. It commemorates, as well, his term in the House as an Illinois Representative from 1847 to 1849.

Congress later placed similar memorials to six other Representatives who achieved the Presidency and who also sat in the Old House Chamber: John Tyler, James K. Polk, Millard Fillmore, Franklin Pierce, James Buchanan, and Andrew Johnson.

In another phase of the restoration program that evokes Statuary Hall's past as House Chamber, gold-fringed red draperies accent its columns—as shown in the 1822 painting (page 32) by Samuel F. B. Morse.

Still other details that recall history and bygone life-styles include the room's four reopened fireplaces, an 1819 engraving of the Declaration of Independence, and a copy of the three-tiered oil-lamp chandelier installed by Architect Latrobe.

Besides its state statues, the Capitol has collected more than 500 other works of art, from portraits and panoramic paintings to individual statues and busts—including those of Presidents, Vice Presidents, Chief Justices, and Indian chiefs.

At every turn you see faces—severe or benign, young or old. They recall a saying by Ralph Waldo Emerson: ". . . there is properly no history, only biography."

Presidential likenesses scattered about the building are the easiest to identify. Some are famous works, like Thomas Sully's paintings of Jefferson and Jackson and the portraits of George Washington by Charles Willson Peale and Gilbert Stuart.

Others record historic events—such as
(Continued on page 104)

IRON GATES *bar entrance to the tomb intended for Washington under the Crypt. It contains the bier on which Lincoln's coffin rested while in the Rotunda.*

IN THE CRYPT, *staff members from the Office of the Architect of the Capitol inspect lighted cases that display photographs of the Capitol's history, construction, and furnishings. A visitor (center) stands near a compass stone, the zero point from which Washington streets are numbered and lettered.*

HOUSE

1. Speaker
2. Congresswomen's Suite
3. House Reception Room
   (Sam Rayburn Room)
4. Committee on Ways and Means
5. Grand Staircase—East
6. Speaker's Rooms
7. Parliamentarian
8. Representatives' Retiring Rooms
9. Speaker's Lobby
10. House Chamber
11. Cloakrooms
12. Committee on Appropriations
13. Grand Staircase—West
14. Minority Whip
15. National Statuary Hall
16. Old House Document Room
17. Minority Leader
18. Prayer Room for
    House and Senate

ROT

Old Sandstone Wall

EAST

RESEARCH BY STEPHAN SCHWARTZ

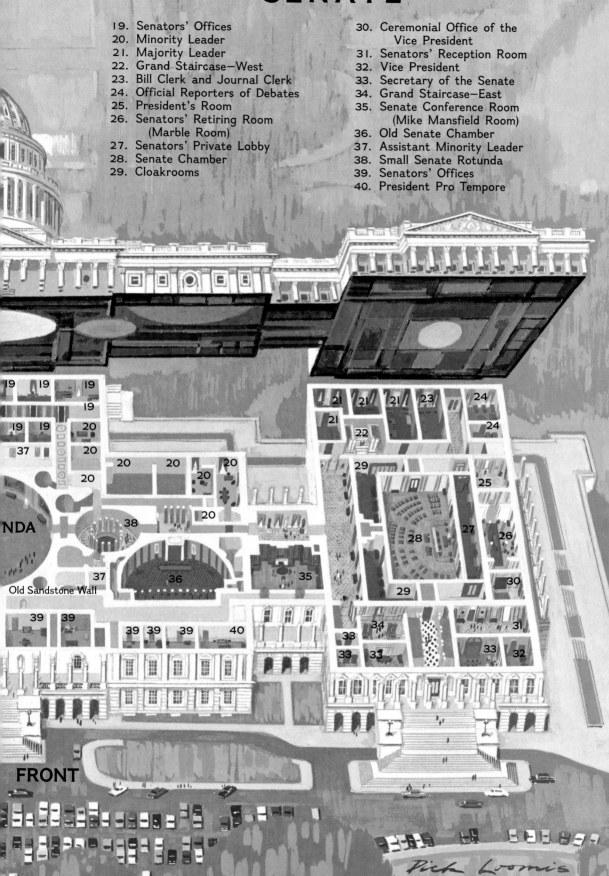

SENATE

(Floor)

19. Senators' Offices
20. Minority Leader
21. Majority Leader
22. Grand Staircase—West
23. Bill Clerk and Journal Clerk
24. Official Reporters of Debates
25. President's Room
26. Senators' Retiring Room
    (Marble Room)
27. Senators' Private Lobby
28. Senate Chamber
29. Cloakrooms

30. Ceremonial Office of the
    Vice President
31. Senators' Reception Room
32. Vice President
33. Secretary of the Senate
34. Grand Staircase—East
35. Senate Conference Room
    (Mike Mansfield Room)
36. Old Senate Chamber
37. Assistant Minority Leader
38. Small Senate Rotunda
39. Senators' Offices
40. President Pro Tempore

NDA

Old Sandstone Wall

FRONT

Rick Loomis

VISITORS' HEADS *create a living frieze around a balustrade in the Senate Rotunda. Architect Latrobe built this vestibule as a light well replacing stairs burned in the British raid of 1814. He gave capitals atop the 16 columns a motif of tobacco flowers and leaves— tribute to the plant's importance in the young Nation's economy.*

NATHANAEL GREENE, *Revolutionary hero, stands in stone in the Capitol— the first statue to be placed after states were invited thus to honor noted citizens.*

Lincoln meeting with his Cabinet to read the Emancipation Proclamation, a scene depicted in the huge painting over the Senate's west stairway. The artist, Francis B. Carpenter, did the painting in the White House; Lincoln himself authenticated details.

Twenty of the busts in the collection of Vice Presidents look out from niches around the walls of the Senate gallery—a reminder that the chief official duty of this office is to preside as President of the Senate.

John Adams, in ruffled stock, is here as Vice President under Washington. Adams was far from pleased by his election. He wrote his wife that his country had arranged for him "the most insignificant office that ever the invention of man contrived."

"I have now . . . 'taken the veil,' " Theodore Roosevelt wrote a friend after his election to the post in 1900.

Chester A. Arthur, also among the 20 busts in the Senate gallery, served as Vice President for only six months in 1881 before Garfield's assassination brought him the Presidency. Political enemies nicknamed him "His Accidency."

Yet despite such witticisms, only two Vice Presidents have ever resigned. John C. Calhoun gave up the office in 1832 to return to the Senate. Spiro T. Agnew, after pleading "no contest" to charges of income-tax evasion, stepped down in 1973.

As for the Indian chiefs, three busts in the Capitol go back to the 1850's, when tribal leaders often traveled to the seat of government to sign land treaties or to seek redress for grievances. Two of these figures represent the same man—a Chippewa chief called Beeshekee, or "the Buffalo." The marble original, displayed in the Senate wing, was sculptured in 1854 by Francis Vincenti. The copy, seen on the House side, was made four years later in the Capitol's bronze shop.

It took diligent detective work about 70 years ago to identify a mysterious third bust, also by Vincenti. It turned out to be that of another Chippewa chief, Aysh-ke-bah-ke-ko-zhay, known as "Flat Mouth."

David Wooster, mortally wounded in 1777 at Ridgefield, Connecticut, inspired Brumidi's mural for a Senate Appropriations Committee room. Hundreds of Brumidi works, large and small, adorn the Capitol.

Even more engaging than the Indian exhibits is an eight-ton block of marble in the Crypt. This monument, surmounted by heads of three stern-looking Victorian ladies, stands amid massive columns and groined arches that support the Rotunda floor above. The work honors a trio of pioneer suffragettes, Lucretia Mott, Elizabeth Cady Stanton, and Susan B. Anthony.

Modern sightseers smile at the group's nickname, the "Ladies in a Bathtub." But there was nothing comic about the gratitude of the many women's organizations that presented the memorial in 1921. In what was perhaps the liveliest celebration the Rotunda ever knew, hundreds of women marched around the room, waving banners in the happy knowledge that they had recently won their long battle for woman suffrage.

One floor below the suffragettes, and beneath the center of the Rotunda, visitors find a tomb—the spot where Congress had hoped to enshrine the body of George Washington. After his death in 1799, Congress passed a joint resolution authorizing a monument to honor the first President at the heart of the future Capitol. His remains were to be transferred from Mount Vernon and placed in a space beneath the monument. But years passed without action.

About 1820, during construction of the central section of the Capitol, a wide circular opening was left in the Rotunda floor to admit light and permit visitors to look down on Washington's monument, as they do in Paris on the Tomb of Napoleon.

"The idea was poetical, grand, and captivating," said John Trumbull. But after his paintings of the Revolution were hung in

GILDED SPLENDOR. *Brumidi frescoes and Minton tiles decorate the Senate Reception Room. Paintings of Robert A. Taft (seen at right), Calhoun, Webster, Clay, and La Follette fill panels Brumidi left vacant. Gathered is the Senate Leadership: (from left) Alan K. Simpson, George J. Mitchell, Robert J. Dole, and Alan Cranston. At left, an 1873 engraving shows the room as the Ladies' Parlor; carpeting hides the intricate tiles.*

men who have lain in state in the Rotunda since 1865.

Come up from the building's gloomy depths to the ground floor of the Senate wing. Here you walk on color, surrounded by more color in the decorative art that covers wall and ceiling surfaces of corridors and committee rooms.

Underfoot, in blue, cream, and red, stretch glazed tiles made in the mid-1850's by skilled craftsmen of England's Minton works. Though millions have trod these tiles, even worn them down in spots, the colors remain amazingly vivid.

On the walls, Brumidi painted in both oil and fresco. Laboring for years, he created incredibly varied designs of birds, animals, flowers, and fruits, interlaced with scrollwork. He drew medallion portraits of many famous Americans, intermingled with battle scenes, landscapes, and panels representing American farming and industry.

Outside the room once used by the Committee on Patents, you see Brumidi's portraits of Benjamin Franklin in his laboratory, and of rival inventors Robert Fulton and John Fitch with early steamboat models.

Stroll along the hall that leads from the Patent Corridor, and you pass more Brumidi paintings, and—for a 20th-century event—a mural by Allyn Cox that depicts the American astronauts making mankind's historic landing on the moon in 1969.

Now turn left on a cross hall, and you return to the past in the restored Supreme
(Continued on page 110)

1824, he found that damp air rising from the Crypt was ruining his work. At Trumbull's urging, Capitol masons closed the floor opening in 1828. Four years later, Washington's heirs finally decided against removing the General's remains from Mount Vernon.

Congress then commissioned Horatio Greenough to make a statue of the Father of His Country. Greenough draped his marble Washington in classic Greek style, a sight that shocked the public when the statue was first displayed in the Rotunda in 1841.

As Capitol Architect Bulfinch had predicted, people wanted "to see the great man as their imagination had painted him." He feared that the statue would "give the idea of entering or leaving a bath." So the heroic 20-ton figure was moved out to the grounds; then, in 1908, it was transferred to the Smithsonian Institution.

Washington's tomb site, however, is not vacant. There you see a black-draped bier, protected from souvenir hunters by an iron gate. On this somber catafalque, first built for Lincoln, have rested the bodies of all the

THE SENATE *convenes for an official portrait on June 12, 1990. Vice President Dan Quayle presides as President of the Senate. He faces the Members from his seat between the flags on the rostrum. Officers of the chamber and pages flank the presiding officer. Democratic Senators sit to his right, Republicans to his left. Unlike the Members of the House, who*

take their seats on benches, the 100 Members of the Senate sit at desks ordered in 1819 or at reproductions of those original 48 desks. Busts of past Vice Presidents occupy the niches in the gallery walls. A Senate resolution permitted the National Geographic Society to record the scene above. Rules generally forbid photography in the chamber.

LACQUERED SNUFFBOXES,
kept filled with fresh snuff though
no longer used, sit on ledges
near the Senate rostrum. Sena-
tor Clay made trips to the boxes
a signal to his followers.

CRYSTAL SHAKER *dispenses*
blotting sand, a heritage of
days when Senators wrote
with quill pens. Today the
desk-top shakers stand
empty, occasionally serving
as paperweights.

Court Chamber off the small Senate Rotunda in the oldest part of the Capitol.

This area, occupied by the Senate from 1800 to 1810, and by the Supreme Court from 1810 to 1860, knew events that rocked the country and helped mold its destiny.

Here, in 1801 and 1805, Jefferson was sworn in as the third U. S. President, and here, in 1857, Chief Justice Roger B. Taney read his opinion in the Dred Scott case, which denied Negroes the right to citizenship and fanned the fires of controversy that soon exploded into the Civil War.

Displaying much of its original furniture and decoration, the court chamber has been restored to its appearance during the mid-19th century. Particularly striking is its half-dome ceiling—the "umbrella vault" designed by Latrobe when he created a much-needed room for Senate sessions in the upper portion of the two-story area.

Even in the days when both the Capitol and the Nation were young, however, the ground-floor space allotted to the high court was uncomfortably crowded.

It was "hardly capacious enough for a ward justice," wrote a New York correspondent in 1824. "... It is a triangular, semicircular, odd-shaped apartment, with three windows, and a profusion of arches. ... Owing to the smallness ... the Judges are compelled to put on their robes in the presence of spectators."

But the cases heard by the court were of national significance, and fashionable Washington found in lawyers' eloquence a substitute for its lack of the glamour and cultural diversions of the big city.

Here Webster in 1819 argued an important constitutional issue involving his alma mater, Dartmouth, and ended with the moving words: "It is, Sir ... a small college and yet there are those who love it."

For today's sightseers, Capitol Architect

SENATE LOBBY recalls rooms of the past where individuals with pet projects buttonholed legislators in attempts to influence legislation. From such anteroom meetings came the term "lobbying." Today, Senators enjoy privacy in their lobby since it ranks as part of the Senate floor, an area where rules limit public access. Clockwise from left are Senators Christopher J. Dodd, Trent Lott, Charles E. Grassley, Richard C. Shelby, Wyche Fowler, Jr., Don Nickles, Paul S. Sarbanes, and Warren B. Rudman.

George M. White and his staff—working with the Senate Commission on Art and Antiquities—have restored the no-less historic Old Senate Chamber above that of the Supreme Court.

Again the room looks as it did in the 1850's. Replicas of desks used then stand in their original spots. The visitors' gallery overlooks the floor, and the same carved and gilded eagle spreads its wings above the chair of the President of the Senate.

In the formative years of the Nation's territorial and economic expansion, this room echoed furious debates over guiding legislation. It heard Senator Thomas Corwin of Ohio make his brave, futile stand in 1847 against popular sentiment for the Mexican War. And it saw Corwin's prophecy come true that acquiring land from Mexico would lead to disastrous sectional strife.

Indeed, it was in this very room, less than ten years later, that Congressional conflict over the extension of slavery in the new western lands reached a climax in the brutal caning of Senator Charles Sumner of Massachusetts by South Carolina Representative Preston S. Brooks.

The Civil War was still an ominous shadow in 1859 when the Senate moved in ceremonial procession to its present chamber in the extended Senate wing.

The following year, the Supreme Court took over the former Senate Chamber, where the Justices would remain for three-quarters of a century before moving on to their own new building nearby.

Meanwhile, Brumidi was continuing his labor of love during the 1860's and early 1870's by creating two of the Capitol's most impressive showrooms, located behind the

MARBLE ROOM
adjoins the Senate Lobby as part of the Senate floor. The decorative ceiling, pilasters, and fluted Corinthian columns of white Italian marble contrast with Tennessee marble walls and wainscoting. The elegant room once served as a private reception area. In the Brumidi Corridor Allyn Cox's mural (right) records mankind's giant leap in 1969, when U. S. astronauts Neil Armstrong and Edwin Aldrin became the first to set foot on the moon.

present Senate Chamber at either end of the Senators' private lobby.

In the President's Room, Brumidi frescoed his own art gallery on square inch after square inch of ceiling and walls. In addition to panels showing the members of Washington's first Cabinet, he painted curlicued designs framing symbolic figures, pensive Madonnas, and happy cherubs.

Though Presidents seldom visit this room now, many Chief Executives, beginning in the 1860's, sat at its oval table, signing 11th-hour bills into law.

Equally ornate is the Senate Reception Room, where Senators meet constituents. But how, you may ask, did portraits of past notables painted in recent times get into the frames made long before by Brumidi?

The story goes back to 1874. "Sooner or later," the artist declared then, the "disfiguring" spaces that remained among his panels "must be completed."

The time came in 1957, when a Special Senate Committee, headed by future President John F. Kennedy, chose five outstanding Senators of the past to be honored by portraits painted in the medallions.

The selection was "nearly an impossible task," Senator Kennedy wrote at the time. In the end the committee recommended five: the "Great Triumvirate," Clay, Webster, and Calhoun, and leaders of later progressive and conservative forces—Robert M. La Follette, Sr., and Robert A. Taft.

Yet there is always something new under the Capitol Dome. Back in 1857 the House of Representatives voted for "plain brown democratic walls" instead of emulating the Senate's more lavish ornamentation.

Then, early in 1970, the nonprofit U. S. Capitol Historical Society offered to donate the necessary funds, together with the talent of Allyn Cox, to produce a series of decorative murals in the House wing. Congress accepted and by midsummer of 1974 the project was completed by Cox and his chief assistant, Cliff Young, with helpers John Roach and Delilah Hoyle.

Visitors to the ground-floor corridors outside the House Restaurant can now look up to vaulted ceilings and see vivid pictures of Capitol personalities and events.

HERE ARE PORTRAITS of Architects of the Capitol and paintings of 13 other buildings where Congress met. Here, too, are eight large murals depicting such scenes as George Washington laying the Capitol's cornerstone, the firing of the building by British invaders in 1814, and the Rotunda when it served as a Civil War hospital.

With Congressional approval, the Society launched the second of its four proposed projects to decorate the halls of the House wing. Funded by the Daughters of the American Revolution, this section was finished in 1983. Its subjects illustrate 300 years of events related to legislation by Congress.

The selection of the Mayflower Compact to introduce this series was based on history's judgment that the accord was a pioneering step toward self-government in what would eventually become the United States.

In his drawing, Mr. Cox pictures the signers of the compact as they gather in the cabin of the Pilgrim ship before landing at Plymouth in 1620.

The agreement itself provided that the quarreling and often divided Mayflower passengers would form a "civill body politick" and abide by the laws adopted for the general good of Plymouth Colony.

THE PRESIDENT'S ROOM, *one of the most ornate chambers in the Capitol, recalls bygone years when the Chief Executive and other dignitaries would gather here for dramatic bill-signing ceremonies. The elaborate frescoes are the work of Brumidi. The portrait in the far wall panel depicts Henry Knox, who served as Secretary of War under George Washington; epaulets recall his combat role during the Revolutionary War. The Madonna-like figures in the ceiling medallions represent religion (left) and executive authority (right).*

By 1982, when muralist Cox died at age 86, he had left a legacy that unrolls a pageant of memorable events. On either side of each historical scene are vignettes that show the human and everyday side of life from that particular era.

Vignettes accompanying the Mayflower Compact portray a woman at her spinning wheel, and an Indian chief as a reminder to us of the original Americans who would meet the arriving immigrants.

Everywhere, in both large and smaller paintings, you see details that give authenticity and vitality to the work.

Clothing, furnishings, and outdoor background all had to be precise in period and situation. Like a sculptor, Cox even studied the physical characteristics of his human subjects to ensure correct height, weight, and proper hang of clothing.

Here, in Benjamin Franklin's garden—where Cox placed delegates discussing the drafting of the Constitution in 1787—you find the slight figure of James Madison beside the aging Franklin. Over there, George Washington (six-feet-two) dominates the scene as he takes the oath of office in 1789 at the temporary capital of New York.

In kaleidoscopic sequence, the paintings attract passing visitors. They see President Monroe and his Cabinet of 1823 devising the far-reaching Monroe Doctrine that would warn European monarchs to keep out of the Western Hemisphere.

They observe Abraham Lincoln, at the East Front of the Capitol in 1865, delivering his second inaugural address—the speech that contained the famous appeal "to bind up the nation's wounds . . . and cherish a just, and a lasting peace. . . ."

Capturing a more flamboyant mood, Cox painted "Teddy" Roosevelt campaigning for the Presidency, while H. L. Mencken and other reporters scribble notes.

Images of a one-room schoolhouse and of a land grant college symbolize American education. The paintings flank a rendering of the Library of Congress when it occupied two floors in the Capitol before moving to the first of its three magnificent buildings.

Early American industry is represented by an 1868 iron foundry with men putting a product through a heat-treatment process.

Vignettes of women factory workers and a cotton gin contribute to the theme of the Industrial Revolution. Across the corridor, a steam-powered boat entering a stream suggests America's transportation expansion by river and canal.

Finally, Cox spotlights the end of an era in a painting of suffragettes parading in 1917—three years before the 19th amendment gave women their nationwide voting rights.

Yet, however beguiling such historic murals and other forms of Capitol art may be,

CEREMONIAL OFFICE *of the Vice President, near the Senate Chamber, affords a quiet moment for Dan Quayle and his wife, Marilyn. Here, more than a century earlier, Vice President Henry Wilson died from a "congestive chill" after tubbing in a Senate bath. Here also, in 1881, Chester A. Arthur repeated the Presidential oath following Garfield's assassination. The mirror and fireplace date from the room's first occupancy in 1859.*

JOHN JAY served as Chief Justice of the United States from 1789 to 1795, after notable contributions to the peace agreement ending the Revolution.

JOHN MARSHALL, *Chief Justice of the United States (1801 to 1835), helped mold the Supreme Court and the Nation with far-reaching opinions.*

sight-seeing visitors come sooner or later to the legislative chambers in which Members of Congress speak and vote.

Those who take the officially guided free tour are admitted in groups to the public galleries looking down on the debaters. Individuals may obtain passes from Representatives or Senators for the asking.

The House Chamber—139 feet long and 93 feet wide—is one of the world's largest legislative rooms. Here Representatives sit in rows of unmarked chairs, as if in a theater without reserved seats. By tradition, however, Republicans group themselves to the Speaker's left and Democrats to his right.

In the smaller Senate Chamber, each Member has an assigned desk. Here too the

OLD SUPREME COURT Chamber, restored for the Bicentennial, contains many original furnishings. Busts of the first Chief Justices look down on the vaulted hall designed by Architect Latrobe. The "pumpkin shell" ceiling, rebuilt after being burned by the British, encloses the room directly beneath the Old Senate Chamber. Beginning in 1810, counselors, including Daniel Webster, argued constitutional cases here. The Supreme Court relocated upstairs (right) after the Senate moved to its present-day quarters in 1859.

CHERUB AND EAGLE grace bronze railings of Members' staircases in both the Senate and House wings. A French artisan, Edmond Baudin, modeled them in 1859 from designs by Brumidi. The latter worked on Capitol decorations through the administrations of six Presidents. Assistants mixed colors, painted backgrounds, or drew preliminary outlines from his sketches, but Brumidi himself finished each of the works.

Republicans and Democrats sit respectively to the left and right of the Vice President. Each desk has an inkwell and a crystal shaker to hold blotting sand—mementos of the quill-pen era. And on ledges flanking the rostrum rest two lacquered snuffboxes, recalling the sneezes that many old-time Senators considered an inducement to clear-headed eloquence. For a modern touch, microphones are now used by the Senators to amplify their remarks and rebuttals.

Visiting constituents, who may wonder at the casual atmosphere or lack of attendance in today's chambers, are reassured to learn that most of the labors of Congress are performed in committees. As Woodrow Wilson wrote, "Congress in session is Congress on public exhibition, whilst Congress in committee-rooms is Congress at work."

Important legislation, however, brings Senators and Representatives hurrying to record their yeas or nays.

When the nuclear test-ban treaty came up for Senate ratification in 1963, all but one of the 100 Senators were in place. The missing Member was seriously ill in a hospital.

But there is still another side to the Capitol, behind the marble miles of showpieces and the public activities of Congress. You find this side in a working world of men and women whose job behind the scenes is to preserve and maintain the vast home of Congress and to keep its legislative mills forever grinding.

BRILLIANT TRACERY draws the attention of visitors in the Brumidi Corridor on the ground floor of the Senate wing. Here the artist painted walls and ceilings with birds, flowers, medallion portraits, and drawings of important inventions. Glazed Minton tile patterns the floor.

The Capitol at Work

"THE CAPITOL is a little city in itself," wrote a knowledgeable Washington newspaperman, Frank G. Carpenter, back in 1883.

It still is, only more so, as Congressional chores and needs expand to meet the increasing demands of modern legislation.

Along corridors of the Capitol traveled by sight-seeing crowds, you can find a post office, railroad ticket office, a book and souvenir shop, cafeterias, and restaurants.

Within the expansive Capitol complex, which includes nearby office buildings, there are carpentry, plumbing, electrical, and machine-repair shops; purchasing offices, warehouses, barbershops, gymnasiums, beauty parlors, libraries, stationery shops, printing offices, and mailing rooms.

A medical staff maintains first-aid and consulting rooms, mainly for Members of Congress, but available to outsiders in case of serious accident, or other emergency. A Capitol police corps, established in 1828 and responsible to a Congressional board, guards the buildings and grounds.

There is a Capitol Prayer Room, voted by a concurrent resolution of House and Senate in 1954. The nondenominational chamber remains open around the clock when Congress is in session. Anonymous donors presented the room's Bible, candelabra, flower vases, U. S. flag, and stained-glass window showing George Washington's kneeling figure.

Many Senators and Representatives come to this room of meditation and prayer. And the number increases, attendants report, when crucial bills are up for decision.

"The late Senator Carter Glass once said that in 28 years he had never known a speech to change a vote," one Member noted. "But I know of several colleagues whose votes changed after visits to our Prayer Room."

Congress's working quarters are scattered from its debating halls to the farthest corners of its office buildings.

Immediately surrounding the formal chambers are the legislators' private lobbies and cloakrooms, while beyond stretch mazes of administrative and clerical offices.

The word "lobbyist" came from such legislative anterooms, in which special pleaders sought to influence lawmakers. The term "lobbying" was current in the Capitol as early as 1832. During the heyday of railway expansion, the practice was so effective that Vermont's Senator Morrill once sarcastically proposed appointing a committee to consult with a railway president waiting in another lobby, to learn whether or not he wished any further legislation.

Rules for admitting outsiders to the floors of House and Senate have varied sharply through the years. During Senate debates on the Missouri Compromise in 1820, gallant Vice President Daniel D. Tompkins invited so many ladies into the chamber that they filled all the available seats and "got literally on the floor, to the no small inconvenience and displeasure of many gentlemen," a commentator reported.

When Congress is in session today, only officially authorized persons may come onto either floor. All others are rigidly excluded —not only from where Congress sits, but from most adjoining rooms as well.

At other times, those who are privileged to visit the empty House and Senate areas see them as stage settings from which the actors

PRAYER ROOM *stays open at all times to legislators from both houses during sessions. Behind the Reverend Richard C. Halverson (left), Senate chaplain, and the Reverend James David Ford, House chaplain, a stained-glass window highlights the figure of George Washington and the 16th Psalm's appeal: "Preserve me, O God, for in Thee do I put my trust." Washington labeled religion and morality "a necessary spring of popular government."*

have temporarily departed. Along the walls of the narrow Speaker's Lobby behind the House Chamber and in the stairwells that adjoin the lobby hang the portraits of 47 Speakers, from Frederick A. C. Muhlenberg to Thomas P. (Tip) O'Neill, Jr.

Muhlenberg of Pennsylvania presided over the infant House of Representatives in 1789, a month before President-elect George Washington was inaugurated. Like many early political leaders, Muhlenberg had served in the Continental Congress. He gave up a career as a Lutheran minister to take part in the affairs of the Nation.

Nathaniel Macon, Speaker in Jefferson's time, called the Speaker "the elect of the elect of all the people."

When you look at Henry Clay's thin, intense face here, you recall the young War Hawk who was chosen to preside on his first day in the House, and who served as Speaker through virtually all of his six terms as a Kentucky Representative.

Strong men in the Speaker's chair have endowed the office with great prestige and immense power to influence legislation.

Studying the portraits of "Czar" Reed and "Uncle Joe" Cannon brings back the eras of the 1890's and early 1900's. These two Speakers were admired and feared for their ruthless exercise of power through committee appointments and other tactics.

The painting of bearded Speaker Cannon looks surprisingly mild for the man who

SENATE MINORITY Leader Robert J. Dole (far right) counsels members of his staff: (from left to right) Deputy Chief of Staff Jim Whittinghill, Administrative Assistant Jim Wholey, and Chief of Staff Sheila Burke. As head of the minority party, the Senator plans floor strategy and guards Republican interests. The Minority Leader's suite, one of the oldest in the Capitol, includes the private office shown here. The suite housed the Supreme Court robing rooms until 1935.

clung fiercely to his dictatorship until a 1910 resolution, pushed through by a rebel coalition, curbed his appointment power.

In Speaker Reed's portrait, painted in 1891 by John S. Sargent, you see a massive, egg-bald man with drooping mustache. Said Reed when he was shown the painting, "All my enemies are revenged."

Portraits of the Speakers are placed in the House lobby after the leaders have left Congress. The painting of former Speaker O'Neill was hung in December 1986.

One of the more recent paintings is that of the man who was Speaker longer than any other in history—Sam Rayburn of Texas.

In 1961, when the able "Mr. Sam" earned the distinction of having presided more than twice as long as Clay, the previous record holder, the House held a special ceremony of congratulations and appreciation.

Dozens of Representatives spoke of Rayburn's parliamentary genius; of his integrity, impartiality, and kindness to new Members; of the bills vital to Americans that he had shepherded into law.

"I trust that those who follow us will know the history of our institutions and keep this Government free," he responded. "It is a tremendous honor for anyone, man or woman, to be elected one time to any office within in the gift of the people."

Located off the main lobby outside the Senate Chamber, the Marble Room is in keeping with the dignity of that formal body.

Variegated Tennessee marble lines the walls; columns of white Italian marble support the ceiling.

At either end of a 64-foot expanse, gilt-framed mirrors repeat rich blue carpets and crystal chandeliers. Magazines and newspapers on mahogany tables heighten the club-room flavor. Senators guard the privacy of their Marble Room—now officially designated part of the chamber itself. But this hall has seen lighter moments.

In earlier times, when pages were younger and authorities more tolerant, the messengers met here, a former Senate page recalled in memoirs published in 1886. Busts of two Indian chiefs adorned the room; on one "venerable Indian head" the group's chief executive "used to sit when presiding."

Next door, the ceremonial office of the Vice President contains a massive desk and an elaborate gilt-framed mirror that reflects a seven-tiered crystal chandelier. The mirror was part of the room's original furnishings when the Senate moved to its new wing in 1859. The chandelier had hung in the White House until the early 1900's. Visitors to the office also see the marble bust of the Vice President under Grant, Henry Wilson, who died here in 1875.

Though Congress is proud of its splendid rooms, lawmaking, after all, is its basic function. And today's legislative work has become so complex that it takes more than 16,000 men and women to help the 540 Members of Congress perform their jobs.

Members have their own office staffs, usually including an administrative assistant and secretarial and clerical help. Each Member has the Congressional Research Service of the Library of Congress to look up information on any subject. And Members can turn to the Office of the Legislative Counsel for help in wording legal fine points of a bill.

The committees that Members may serve on—Congress has 38 standing committees plus hundreds of subcommittees—employ batteries of technical people to advise on anything from flood control to space flight. In addition, the Senate and House have legislative and administrative staffs—headed by the Secretary of the Senate and Clerk of the House—that include document superintendents, financial clerks, librarians, and oth-

ers. Their knowledge of Congressional functions and traditions is essential.

Yet despite such assistance, only Members can attend to many matters. They must see visiting constituents, gather information, and perform other services for state and business interests back home. Responding to letters is a big item.

More than 200 million letters and other pieces of mail pour into the Capitol complex annually. Constituents may ask for help with problems involving Social Security or welfare benefits, a Government job, or advice on how to find a runaway spouse or child. A would-be inventor once asked his Congressman to send him a list of everything that had not yet been invented.

Letters may contain bouquets of praise.

SENATE APPROPRIATIONS COMMITTEE *reviews the allocation of revenues for executive agencies and federal spending programs. The Members meet in a room originally decorated for the old Senate Committee on Naval Affairs. Nine large panels painted in oil feature mythological marine divinities in flowing robes. Twenty-nine Members constitute the Senate Appropriations Committee, which is divided into 13 subcommittees. Seated (counterclockwise from front) are Senators Wyche Fowler, Jr., Brock Adams, Harry Reid, Tom Harkin, Frank R. Lautenberg, Dale Bumpers, Dennis DeConcini, Jim Sasser, Warren B. Rudman, Arlen Specter, Pete V. Domenici, Charles E. Grassley, Don Nickles, Robert W. Kasten, Jr., Thad Cochran, E. J. (Jake) Garn, James A. McClure, Ted Stevens, Mark O. Hatfield, Robert C. Byrd, Daniel K. Inouye, Ernest F. Hollings, J. Bennett Johnston, Quentin N. Burdick, Patrick J. Leahy, and J. Robert Kerrey. Members not pictured here are Alfonse M. D'Amato, Phil Gramm, and Barbara A. Mikulski.*

STATELY ELEGANCE *marks the office of the Speaker of the House. As the chamber's presiding officer, he wields imposing power in molding legislation. Speaker Thomas S. Foley (center) confers with aides (from left) Werner Brandt, Heather Foley, Mimi McGee O'Hara, and George Kundanis.*

CRYSTAL CHANDELIERS *embellish the offices of the Majority and Minority Leaders of the House. These party chiefs play key roles in directing legislative strategy. They are aided in floor duties by Members called party whips. Majority Leader Richard A. Gephardt (standing at left in opposite photograph) and Minority Leader Robert H. Michel (third from left, far right photograph) meet with their staff members.*

Or more frequently, brickbats. Occasionally, the temptation to talk back is overwhelming. One Representative contented himself with two words in replying to an irate constituent who had threatened to move to Canada. "Bon voyage," he wrote.

Another part of the job is the time-honored practice of sending out Government bulletins on subjects ranging from farm machinery and baby care to gun control, drug abuse, and nuclear energy.

As sessions of Congress run longer and longer, Members lean heavily on modern communications to keep in touch with the people back home. One device is the informal newsletter on events in Washington.

For other home-front links, the Capitol houses radio and TV recording facilities for legislators to use at cost. In convenient studios, Members prepare their reports to

constituents. The tapes and films go to local broadcast stations.

With all these activities, Members have crowded schedules. In the early years of this century, Congress sometimes met for only nine months of the 24-month session. Mail then concerned mostly personal and routine interests, such as free-seed distribution, rural routes, pensions—and now and again some special piece of legislation.

Today, the Members meet almost continuously and consider masses of legislation suggested in Presidential messages, Government-department reports, or petitions from private groups or individuals. They must be ready to defend voting stands to constituents who have greater access than ever before to information.

You could write a book (people have) on how a proposal becomes law, sometimes by

more than 20 stages. The House and Senate go about the business differently. But, shorn of details, the basic steps are these: A House Member drafts a bill—say, one on energy— and drops it into the Clerk's "hopper." The Parliamentarian picks up the bill and refers it to the appropriate House authority—in this case the Committee on Energy and Commerce.

The subcommittee considers the measure. Consultants may be called in, from the Department of Energy or the Department of Transportation, for example. The panel may hold public hearings at which representatives of the oil industry or of federal agencies involved may present their views.

Hearings on important and controversial measures attract intensive news coverage. So do the investigative hearings the Congressional committees undertake. These need

not stem from consideration of the bill. They can result from a need to look into an issue involving Congress's "watchdog" function, which has been since World War II a powerful and much-used tool.

Action at subcommittee and full committee levels may shape the energy bill for return to the House, which puts it on the proper calendar of business. Or, the bill may die in committee.

Of the more than 11,000 measures introduced in the One Hundredth Congress (1987-1989), only 761 became law. Woodrow Wilson wrote that a bill killed in committee has crossed "a parliamentary bridge of sighs. . . . The means and time of its death are unknown, but its friends never see it again."

A bill put on the calendar usually comes up for debate. Discussion may be routine; committee work by party leaders often governs

HOUSE ADMINISTRATION COMMITTEE *sets policy for the management of the internal administrative and operating functions of the House. The committee also oversees the Federal Election Campaign Act and the Contested Election Statute. These laws, respectively, regulate funding of Presidential and Congressional campaigns and govern the disposition of contested election cases. At the table clockwise from front: Reps. Sam Gejdenson, Jim Bates, Al Swift, Leon E. Panetta, Joseph M. Gaydos, staff director David C. Sharman, Chairman Frank Annunzio, Rep. Bill Frenzel, minority staff director Linda Nave, Reps. William L. Dickinson, Robert E. Badham, William M. Thomas, Barbara F. Vucanovich, and Pat Roberts.*

occasionally do—talk around the clock. In both houses, everything said is recorded by official reporters. They work at the bottom dais of the rostrum, or move near the speakers to catch every phrase.

In the days of steel pen points, some stenographers worked with tiny ink bottles strapped to their wrists. Today, House and Senate reporters use either pen-written or machine shorthand to record the proceedings verbatim. House stenographers write in 15-minute relays, those of the Senate in 10-minute stretches.

The short intervals are necessary to maintain the remarkable speed with which statements are recorded. In about 45 minutes complete transcriptions are available to the Members for approval or correction, then sent nightly to the Government Printing Office for inclusion in the next morning's edition of the *Congressional Record*.

This publication, founded in 1873, is an official report of what takes place during the floor sessions. The *Record* has a daily circulation of 30,000. It is bound in paperback every day, and in hardback annually. In the *Record* have long appeared not only speeches actually made, but also extraneous material of all kinds, such as poetry, recipes, or dull statistics that Members may insert in the *Extensions of Remarks*.

Speaker Champ Clark disapproved of printing undelivered speeches and articles, but concluded "it was preferable . . . rather than be compelled to listen to them."

Congress now requires that inserted material be labeled by a large typographic dot, or "bullet." Though this action does not delete irrelevant subjects, the *Record* gives much useful information, especially on bills going through reading, debate, or amendment.

After a measure is passed by the House, it is sent to the Senate for another round of study, debate, and voting. Differences between the House and Senate may be accepted by the originating body, or they may be worked out by committees from the two chambers. Either house may originate a bill, with the Constitutional exception that all the revenue measures begin in the House.

Once approved by the Senate and House, the bill goes to the President. His signature

the bill's fate. Or debate may include oratory ranging from dull to inspired, and orators from little noted to long remembered.

Felix Walker, a legislator of the 1820's, was known as "old oil-jug" because of his many flowing speeches dedicated to Buncombe County in his North Carolina district. Out of those flowery references to his home district came such additions to the language as "bunk," "bunkum," and "debunking."

House rules now limit debate, usually to one hour. Senators are privileged to—and

(Continued on page 135)

CAPITOL POLICE *units range from plainclothesmen to a K-9 explosive detection team. Commanded by Chief Frank A. Kerrigan (front row, far right) and Assistant Chief Harry B. Grevey (front row, far left), the force of more than 1,200 comes under the direction of the Capitol Police Board. This consists of (front row center, left to right) Senate Sergeant at Arms Henry Giugni, Architect of the Capitol George M. White, and House Sergeant at Arms Jack Russ.*

HOUSE TV CONTROL ROOM *monitors sessions on the floor of the House of Representatives and beams the proceedings via cable television to more than seven million homes across the Nation. Six cameras cover House activities, televised since 1979. Rep. Charles Rose pauses at a console called the character generator. An operator working the keyboard helps the viewing audience identify a Representative on camera by displaying the Member's name across the television screen.*

132

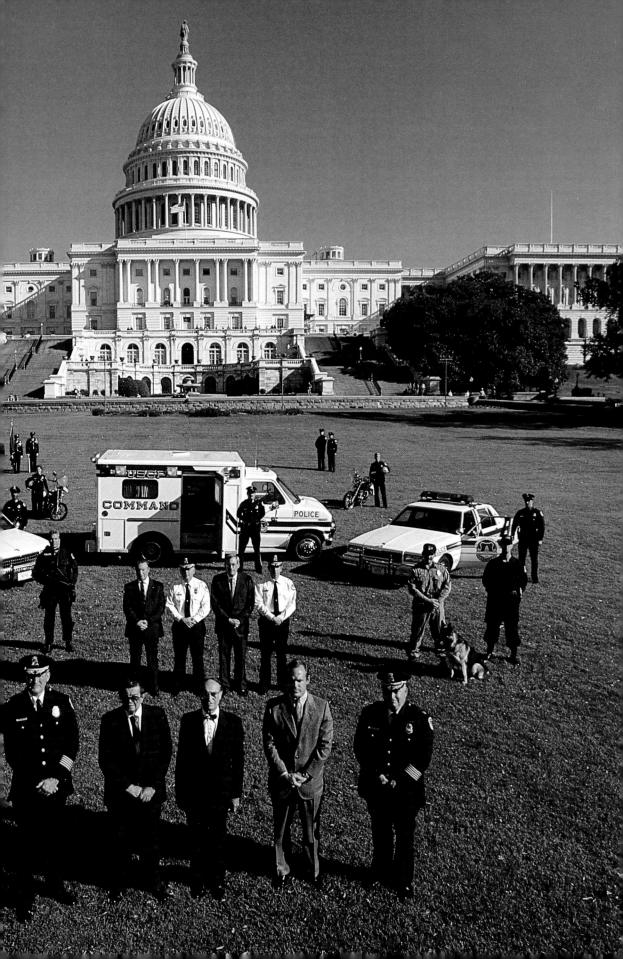

POST OFFICE *and other services give the Capitol the facilities of a small city.*

HOUSE DOCUMENT ROOM *supplies copies of current bills to Representatives.*

BANKING SERVICES *are offered at the House Sergeant at Arms' office, visited here by Reps. Stokes and White.*

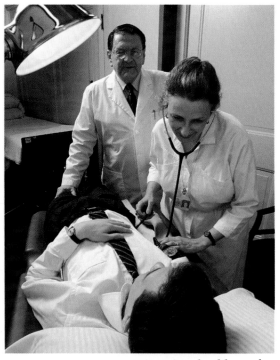

CAPITOL PHYSICIANS *monitor health needs. Dr. William Narva and nurse Katy Como check a page's blood pressure.*

SUBWAYS *provide a quick passage from Senate and House offices to the Capitol.*

makes the bill the law of the land. Should he veto it, the bill can still be enacted by a two-thirds vote of both houses.

From the galleries, visitors see the surface pageantry of this complex process. Moreover, since 1979, the public at large also has had a chance to see a show that has created a new cult of Congress-watchers.

In spring of that year, the House authorized the launching of the first live radio and television coverage of proceedings on the House floor.

Today, broadcasts by the Cable Satellite Public Affairs Network (C-SPAN) give audiences across the Nation a firsthand look at the behavior of their elected Representatives in action.

One avid viewer told a reporter that she now tunes in every day on House debates instead of following her favorite soap operas.

Yet, despite watchers who rated the House show educational and even fascinating, the more conservative Senate did not allow broadcasting until June 1986.

In the ordinary procedures of both houses, the work day starts in the respective chambers when the Speaker of the House and the President of the Senate call the sessions to order, usually at 12 noon. Chaplains offer a prayer. Clerks read bills and record votes.

Parliamentarians advise on rules and precedent. Members who hold the important posts of Majority and Minority Leaders and Whips direct political strategy in carrying out their parties' legislative programs.

Just learning how Congress conducts its business is an undertaking in itself. Freshman legislators, old hands say, need at least a full session merely to grasp the rules and customs they must follow. As Speaker Clark put it, "A new Congressman must begin at the foot of the class and spell up."

When Congress is in session, no offices are busier behind the scenes than each chamber's Document Room. Through these rooms flow endless streams of bills that may range from a proposal for tax reform to a suggestion for a national week in honor of country music. All subjects are indexed, filed, and kept up to date as action is taken.

Distributing current bills from the Document Rooms is the daily responsibility of the Capitol's youngest workers, the Congressional pages. The House employs 66 of these messengers and the Senate 30. Girls began serving as pages when the all-male tradition ended in 1971.

It is the job of the pages to see that legislators' desks are supplied with the necessary materials and that the Senate snuffboxes are properly filled, as well as to run errands during sessions.

The House began using messengers in 1789. Daniel Webster is credited with appointing the first Senate page in 1829; he was nine-year-old Grafton Hanson, a descendant of John Hanson, president of the Continental Congress. Today pages are older (they must be at least juniors in high school), but they still are chosen by the legislators.

The job is no sinecure. Before work, pages must attend accredited page schools in the Library of Congress. Classes begin as early as 6:10 a.m. Courses prepare the students for college through studies devoted to social science, English, foreign languages, mathematics, physics, and chemistry.

U NLIKE PAGES, who work directly for Members of Congress, the Capitol police force has become a professional rather than a patronage organization. The force, which began with a single night watchman employed in 1801, now has 1,200 members, including 160 women.

Routine duties call for a delicate balance. The police corps must protect Members, their staffs, and visiting heads of state and other dignitaries and at the same time guard the right of citizens to have access to their elected representatives. With personnel divided into three daily work shifts, the Capitol police maintain round-the-clock security, seven days a week, for the 40-block, 250-acre complex of Congressional buildings.

Occasionally the job can become more than routine. The force has had to deal with disturbances ranging from minor incidents to destructive political violence. The most dramatic of these events occurred in 1954 when four Puerto Rican nationalists opened fire from the gallery into the House Chamber below. Five Representatives were wounded.

In 1971, a bomb exploded in a men's room in the old Senate wing. The blast caused extensive damage, but no injuries, probably because it went off about 1:30 a.m. In November 1983, another bomb explosion, this time in a second-floor corridor not far from the Senate Chamber, resulted in consider-

GENERAL WASHINGTON *receives a British officer at Yorktown, where victory assured American independence. This historic scene, painted in 1857 by Brumidi, originally adorned the House Chamber. Today the restored fresco graces the House Restaurant. On the briefcase strap at lower right the artist, proud of his adopted country, lettered his signature note, "Citizen of the U. S."*

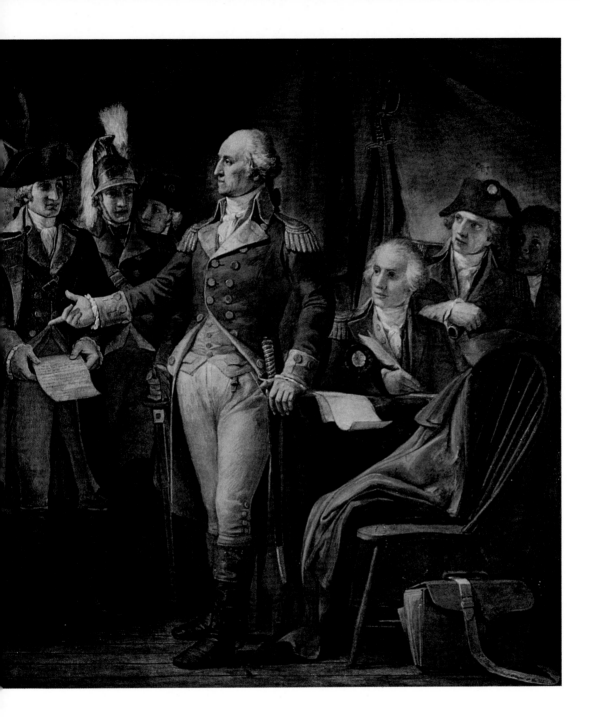

able damage but, again, no casualties. Reacting to such outbreaks and to increasing terrorism around the world, the Capitol police force has formed units specially trained to respond to hazardous devices and barricade or hostage situations.

The Capitol's normal security regulations have also been sharply upgraded. The plaza has been closed to parking, and concrete obstacles and hydraulic barriers have been installed to prohibit entry by unauthorized vehicles. Visitors on foot enter the Capitol only at specified doors, where they walk through metal-detector gates like those used at airports. Visitors are also asked to turn over hand-carried baggage for electronic scanning. A similar procedure is used at the House and Senate galleries.

Such vigilance underscores the importance of the Capitol, a source of world news. Some 2,800 newspaper and periodical correspondents and photographers, plus more

than 1,300 radio and television reporters, are accredited to cover events.

Opportunities to report on Congress have grown steadily in modern word and picture facilities. Early press coverage was not only limited, but often personally and politically abusive. At times, frustrated editors and furious Congressmen indulged in mutual recriminations. Congress was interfering with the rights of a free press, said James Gordon Bennett of the New York *Herald* in 1841. Correspondents were "miserable slanderers," roared a disgruntled Senator.

In more decorous and useful ways, however, the past has a way of cropping up here in the form of valuable historic documents.

CAPITOL'S WEST FRONT *breaks the easy slope of Jenkins Hill. At upper left, the Russell, Dirksen, and Hart buildings provide office space for the Senate. The columned Supreme Court Building rises behind the Capitol near the cupola-capped Library of Congress. House office buildings at right face the Capitol grounds. A similar scene photographed in 1930 (opposite) points up architectural changes made over the decades.*

One, found in a storeroom of the House, was a copy of the bill declaring war against Great Britain in 1812. Another was a cache of brittle, yellowed papers tucked in a cabinet of a Senate attic. Some of them were signed "G? Washington," "John Adams," and "yr. mo. ob. serv. Th: Jefferson."

Such incidents remind us that the Capitol has been a living stage for national events ever since its first small wing was occupied in November of 1800. Its drama-filled past is one of the reasons that visitors find the building so fascinating, and that novelists, playwrights, and filmmakers go to its archives to take real-life plots from American history.

One documentary film, *City Out of Wilderness: Washington* (produced by the U. S. Capitol Historical Society), shows in graphic sequence how the Capitol has reflected the adventures and progress of the Nation during its first two centuries of life.

Through its burning by the British in the War of 1812, through the trauma of the Civil War, two world wars, and the periodic scourge of devastating economic woes, the lawmakers' home has remained an integral force in the making of a federal metropolis and the rise of a great world power.

"What is left for man to do?" asked former Congressman and well-known journalist Henry Watterson in 1919. "With wireless telegraphy, the airplane and the automobile annihilating time and space, what else?"

Some of the answers to that perennial challenge will doubtless be heard within this building where "We, the People" speak.

CAPITOL DOME *and the Washington Monument pierce the horizon at*

dusk. Floodlights define the Lincoln Memorial behind the monument.

Index

PRINTED AND BOUND BY HOLLADAY-TYLER PRINTING CORP.; GLENN DALE, MARYLAND.

Congress OF THE United

begun and held at the City of New-York,

Wednesday the fourth of March, one thousand and seven hund___

THE Conventions of a number of the States, having at the time of their ad___ or abuse of its powers, that further declaratory and restrictive clauses should be added: And as ex_tending the ground of public confid___ RESOLVED by the Senate and House of Representatives of the ___ concurring that the following Articles be proposed to the Legislatures of the several States, as amendments to the Constitution of the U___ said Legislatures, to be valid to all intents and purposes, as part of the said Constitution; viz.

ARTICLES in addition to, and Amendment of the Constitution of the of the several States, pursuant to the fifth Article of the original Constitution.

Article the first..... After the first enumeration required by the first Article of the Constitution, there shall be one Representative for eve ___which, the proportion shall be so regulated by Congress, that there shall be not less than one hundred Rep___ until the number of Representatives shall amount to two hundred, after which the proportion shall be so regula___ nor more than one Representative for every fifty thousand persons.

Article the second... No law, varying the compensation for the services of the Senators and Representatives, shall take effect, until an ___

Article the third...... Congress shall make no law respecting an establishment of religion, or prohibiting the free exercise thereof; or abridg___ assemble, and to petition the Government for a redress of grievances.

Article the fourth. A well regulated Militia, being necessary to the security of a free State, the right of the people to keep and be___

Article the fifth....... No Soldier shall, in time of peace be quartered in any house, without the consent of the Owner; nor in time of war___

Article the sixth...... The right of the people to be secure in their persons, houses, papers, and effects, against unreasonable searches___ probable cause, supported by oath or affirmation, and particularly describing the place to be searched, and the___

Article the seventh... No person shall be held to answer for a capital, or otherwise infamous crime, unless on a presentment or indictment of___ Militia, when in actual service in time of War or public danger; nor shall any person be subject for the same offe___ criminal case to be a witness against himself; nor be deprived of life, liberty, or property, without due process of___

Article the eighth. In all criminal prosecutions, the accused shall enjoy the right to a speedy and public trial, by an impartial ju___ district shall have been previously ascertained by law, and to be informed of the nature and cause of the accusatio___ for obtaining witnesses in his favor, and to have the assistance of Counsel for his defence.

Article the ninth. In suits at common law, where the value in controversy shall exceed twenty dollars, the right of trial by jury sha___ any Court of the United States, than according to the rules of the common law.

Article the tenth. Excessive bail shall not be required, nor excessive fines imposed, nor cruel and unusual punishments inflic___

Article the eleventh. The enumeration in the Constitution, of certain rights, shall not be construed to deny or disparage others retai___

Article the twelfth. The powers not delegated to the United States by the Constitution, nor prohibited by it to the States, are rese___

ATTEST,

Frederick Augustus Muhlenberg Speaker of the Ho___

John Adams Vice-President

John Beckley, Clerk of the House of Representatives.

Sam. A. Otis Secretary of the Senate.